Saltwater Fish as Pets

A Complete Pet Owner's Guide

Facts & Information: Diseases, aquarium, identification, supplies, species, acclimating, food, care, compatibility, tank setup, beginner, buying all covered and more.

By: Lolly Brown

Copyrights and Trademarks

All rights reserved. No part of this book may be reproduced or transformed in any form or by any means, graphic, electronic, or mechanical, including photocopying, recording, taping, or by any information storage retrieval system, without the written permission of the author.

This publication is Copyright © 2013. All products, graphics, publications, software and services mentioned and recommended in this publication are protected by trademarks. In such instance, all trademarks & copyright belong to the respective owners.

Disclaimer and Legal Notice

This product is not legal, medical, or accounting advice and should not be interpreted in that manner. You need to do your own due-diligence to determine if the content of this product is right for you. While every attempt has been made to verify the information shared in this publication, neither the author, neither publisher, nor the affiliates assume any responsibility for errors, omissions or contrary interpretation of the subject matter herein. Any perceived slights to any specific person(s) or organization(s) are purely unintentional.

We have no control over the nature, content and availability of the web sites listed in this book. The inclusion of any web site links does not necessarily imply a recommendation or endorse the views expressed within them. We take no responsibility for, and will not be liable for, the websites being temporarily unavailable or being removed from the internet.

The accuracy and completeness of information provided herein and opinions stated herein are not guaranteed or warranted to produce any particular results, and the advice and strategies, contained herein may not be suitable for every individual. Neither the author nor the publisher shall be liable for any loss incurred as a consequence of the use and application, directly or indirectly, of any information presented in this work. This publication is designed to provide information in regard to the subject matter covered.

Neither the author nor the publisher assume any responsibility for any errors or omissions, nor do they represent or warrant that the ideas, information, actions, plans, suggestions contained in this book is in all cases accurate. It is the reader's responsibility to find advice before putting anything written in this book into practice. The information in this book is not intended to serve as legal, medical, or accounting advice.

Foreword

Any discussion of keeping a saltwater aquarium gets out of hand — fast. Saltwater aquarists aren't casual hobbyists. They are dedicated enthusiasts.

In this text, I have worked to give you a complete and comprehensive foundation to what can become a life's avocation. Be assured of one fact, however. If you keep saltwater fish for 20 years, you will continue to learn new things every day.

For many marine aquarists that is the great appeal of this complex and fascinating pastime. Frankly, most saltwater fish keepers adopt a philosophy of, "go big or go home."

These are not your average tanks, and since it's easier to maintain good water chemistry in a bigger aquarium, don't be intimidated and pick a tank you'll only by replacing in six months when you are more confident and even more enthusiastic.

Your marine tank will teach you patience if this is not a quality you already possess. Almost nothing beneficial ever happens fast in a marine aquarium. Generally, speed equals disaster.

Assume that you will get what you pay for. Budget for quality equipment rather than "saving" money over and over with replacements. Understand from the beginning

Foreword

that some of the fish you may keep can live 20 years and more.

If you are paying upwards to $300 (£188) for one fish, it makes no sense to put the animal in an inferior habitat, or to fail to maintain the life-sustaining environment on which it will depend.

Expect to draw deeply on your skills of engineering and management. You'll find yourself designing, refining, augmenting and monitoring your system for what should be many pleasurable hours. With modern computerized systems, you can even check in on your tank via smartphone.

Freshwater tanks can be fun and beautiful additions to your home. A saltwater tank is an engrossing addition to your life. It is little wonder that saltwater aquarists form a tight and thriving online community, to which you will find yourself turning for impassioned discussions and valuable advice.

The goal of any tank is to define parameters that can be maintained in healthy stasis — temperature, salinity, and water flow among other. You will be responsible for creating a peacefully co-existing community in a closed environment over which your powers — for good and ill — approach god-like proportions.

If you do not have the time, the funds, and above all the commitment to do that, keeping a saltwater tank may not

Foreword

be right for you. But if you are already intrigued by the very prospect, read on. You could well be embarking on an adventure whose path you will happily follow for years to come.

Foreword

Acknowledgments

I would like to express my gratitude towards my family, friends, and colleagues for their kind co-operation and encouragement which helped me in completion of this book.

I would like to express my special gratitude and thanks to my loving husband for his patience, understanding, and support.

My thanks and appreciations also go to my colleagues and people who have willingly helped me out with their abilities.

Additional thanks to my children, whose love and care for our family pets inspired me to write this book.

Acknowledgments

Table of Contents

Foreword 1

Acknowledgments 5

Table of Contents 7

Part I – Designing Your Aquarium Habitat 13

   Weight is a Primary Consideration 13

   Pick a Tank Type 16

      Fish Only (FO) 16

      Fish Only with Live Rock (FOWLR) 16

      Reef Tank 17

   Selecting Your Equipment 18

      Tank Size and Material 18

      Protein Skimmer 19

      Pumps or Powerheads 20

      Salt 21

      Reverse Osmosis De-Ionization 21

      Lighting 23

      Substrate and Rock 23

      Heaters and Chillers 25

      Equipment to Monitor Water Quality 26

      Sump 28

      Auto Top Off 29

Table of Contents

    Backup Generator 29

        Overflow Box 30

    Installing Tank Components 30

    Understanding Basic Water Chemistry 31

        Water Parameters by Tank Type 33

    Cycling Your Tank 35

Estimated Setup Costs 36

Part II – Populating Your Saltwater Tank 41

    Things to Consider Before You Buy 41

    Terms Used to Describe Fish 43

    Buying Healthy Fish 45

    Best Fish Lists? 46

    For Beginners 46

        Damselfish 46

        Clownfish 47

        Blue Green Chromis 47

        Firefish 47

        Kaudern's Cardinal Fish 48

    For Fish Only Tanks 48

        Eels 49

        Groupers 51

        Soldierfish 52

Table of Contents

Puffers 54

Lionfish 55

Larger Angels 56

Butterfly Fish 58

Largers Wrasses 60

Trigger Fish 62

Parrot Fish 62

Tangs 63

Surgeon Fish 64

Rabbit Fish 66

Boxfish 67

Mandarins 69

Squirrelfish 70

Batfish 71

Blennies 72

Moderate to Advanced Tanks 73

Basslets 73

Seahorses 74

Filefish 75

Gobies 75

Reef Tanks 76

Invertebrates 76

Table of Contents

Coral 77

Acclimatization Techniques 77

    Floating Acclimatization 78

    Drip Acclimatization 79

    Dealing with Aggression 81

    Acclimatization Tips 82

Part III – Overview of Saltwater Tank Care 83

    Feeding Your Saltwater Fish 84

        Carnivores 84

        Herbivores 85

        Omnivores 85

    Types of Fish Food 86

    How and When to Feed 88

    Cleaning Chores and Maintenance 89

        Daily Maintenance 90

        Weekly / 10 Days 91

        Monthly 91

    Dealing with Emergencies 92

Part IV – Saltwater Fish Health 95

    Signs of Disease 95

    Your Tank's "First Aid" Kit 97

    Common Disease and Conditions 99

Table of Contents

- Parasites 99
- Bacterial and Fungal Disease 101
- Viral Diseases 104
- Worm Infestations 106
- Medications and Treatments 107
- A Word About Veterinarians 108

Afterword 111

Relevant Websites 113

Frequently Asked Questions 115

Glossary 121

Index 129

Table of Contents

Part I – Designing Your Aquarium Habitat

Part I – Designing Your Aquarium Habitat

It's almost a given that a saltwater aquarist will get bitten by the "bigger is better" bug. Certainly more tank space will allow you to keep a greater variety of larger fish and other aquarium inhabitants. It's a mistake, however, to think about tank size first, without considering exactly where the aquarium will be placed, and what type of tank you want to cultivate.

Weight is a Primary Consideration

It is important not just to think in terms of the volume of your future tank, but what that volume translates to in terms of weight. Let's consider a 180 gallon (681.37 liter) tank with dimensions of 6' x 2' x 2' (1.8m x 0.6m x 0.6m).

Part I – Designing Your Aquarium Habitat

As a standard rule of thumb, you can stock 1 inch (2.54 cm) of adult fish per 5 gallons (18.9 liters) of water. Depending on the size of fish you pick, you have 36 inches (91.44 cm) with which to play. That's more than enough room to create an interesting environment.

You could easily stock your tank with:

8 Green Chromis
(1-2 inches / 2.54-5.08 cm)
Total: 8-16 inches / 20.32-40.64cm

2 Pearlscale Butterflyfish
(2-3 inches / 5.08-7.62cm)
Total: 4-6 inches / 10.16-15.24cm

1 Coral Beauty Angelfish
(2-3 inches / 5.08-7.62cm)
Total: 2-3 inches / 5.08-7.62cm

1 Pacific Blue Tang
(2-3 inches / 5.08-7.62cm)
Total: 2-3 inches / 5.08-7.62cm

1 Clownfish
(1-3 inches / 2.54-7.62cm)
Total: 1-3 inches / 2.54-7.62cm

Tank Total: 17-31 inches / 43.18-78.74cm

Part I – Designing Your Aquarium Habitat

Truth be told, most tanks are always just a tad overstocked, so you could throw in a few more small fish.

That all sounds great, right? Well, here's the reality test. Your tank is going to weigh 1,440 lbs. / 653.17 kg.

The bigger you go, the heavier you go. Then you start having to think about your home or office and start asking purely structural questions.

- Will the tank be suitable for a second story?
- Are my floors reinforced?
- Can they be reinforced? (This can even be true of a lower floor.)
- Will the tank have to sit directly on concrete?

It is certainly not unheard of for a saltwater enthusiast to remodel a portion of their home to accommodate a new and larger aquarium, but you don't want to start out your new hobby by having to hire an engineer and an architect to make it work.

Pick a tank size that can be placed in your existing home or office. Learn everything there is to know about maintaining a saltwater aquarium with that first tank.

Make all your mistakes on a reasonable scale, because making them on an enormous scale gets very expensive very quickly.

Part I – Designing Your Aquarium Habitat

Pick a Tank Type

There are three basic configurations for saltwater tanks:

- fish only
- fish only with live rock
- reef

The requirements for setup and maintenance, as well as the potential for stocking the population, vary with each configuration.

Fish Only (FO)

Fish only aquariums are exactly what the name suggests, tanks that are set up to house marine fish as the focal point of the display, often with few decorations beyond replica coral.

They are excellent tanks for people new to marine aquariums, and will allow you to learn about the necessary equipment, water chemistry, and population management.

Fish Only with Live Rock (FOWLR)

The natural progression in this hobby is to start with a fish only tank, and to move up to a FOWLR tank as a bridge toward eventually having a reef tank. FOWLR aquariums incorporate live rock, which are fragments of coral reefs that come with natural colonies of marine life.

Part I – Designing Your Aquarium Habitat

This will include invertebrates, sponges, and lots and lots of beneficial nitrifying bacteria. The rock is fantastic secondary filtration and goes a long way toward creating more stable water, not to mention the realistic undersea aesthetic it adds to a tank.

Clownfish

There are, of course, additional considerations for acclimatizing and caring for the live rock, especially in terms of correct lighting and supplements. Additionally, you will have to be more careful not to harm the bacteria by putting any kind of chemicals like medications in the water.

Reef Tank

There are two words typically associated with reef tanks: expensive and challenging. You may have very few fish or

Part I – Designing Your Aquarium Habitat

none at all in a reef tank, but you will have lots of corals and invertebrates. These creatures are highly sensitive to water condition, so you will face the challenge of maintaining chemically stable water at the highest level.

Corals are photosynthetic. Without the right lighting, they won't live. Pretty much everything in a reef tank needs special attention, but for the people who keep them, and who thrive on that level of fine detail, there's no more satisfying kind of tank.

Selecting Your Equipment

When you've made a determination on the size aquarium you can handle relative to your home or office, and then chosen a type of tank to install, you can begin to select your equipment. The following is an overview of the major components of a basic marine tank.

Tank Size and Material

We've already discussed the factors of size and weight. Go with the largest tank you can afford and house. At minimum for a marine tank, you want to start in the 30-55 gallon (113.56-208.2 liter) range.

With water alone weighing 8 pounds (3.62 kg), you're looking at a minimum tank weight of 240-440 pounds (100-200 kg). If possible, start at the 180 gallon (681.37 liter) level. This will give you far more options, and will actually be easier to maintain even for a beginner.

Part I – Designing Your Aquarium Habitat

(Please note that all of our examples and estimated prices for equipment are based on a 180 gallon / 681.37 liter tank size.)

Estimated Cost:
180 gallon / 681.37 liter tank
$350 / £223

For the most part, the choice of a glass tank over an acrylic one is a matter of personal preference. Glass tanks come in typical rectangular shapes, while custom tanks are frequently made of acrylic to achieve unique shapes.

Acrylic does scratch easily, so all equipment must be rated "acrylic safe." Glass will crack, break, or shatter if hit with sufficient force, and acrylic is much more durable.

However, glass is the easier of the two to support. If you have an acrylic tank, you must purchase a stand with full-bottom support to prevent bowing or splitting.

Glass is thicker, and tends to distort both position and color. These effects are greatly lessened when looking through acrylic, however, glass is clear, and acrylic does have a tendency to yellow over time.

Protein Skimmer

Protein skimmers create bubbles inside a reaction chamber. Waste materials in the water attach themselves to the bubbles, which rise to the surface and pass into a collection

Part I – Designing Your Aquarium Habitat

cup where the waste remains. This cup needs to be emptied daily.

In addition to serving a maintenance function, the bubbles are another source of oxygenation, which contributes to a more stable level of pH in the water.

Larger protein skimmers operate more efficiently and thus make your aquarium easier to keep. Always buy the largest skimmer you can afford in relation to the size of your tank.

Estimated Cost:
$350 / £223

Pumps or Powerheads

The devices that circulate water in your aquarium are called either pumps or powerheads.

Your goal is to hit a target "turnover rate" or "flow rate," which will vary by tank size and type. The number will likely be 6-10 times per hour. Expect to see the capacity of these items listed in terms of gallons per hour (GPH) or liters per hour (LPH).

Unless you are housing species that might be sensitive to too much flow in the water, it's generally best to err on the side of more water movement.

(As you come to understand the design of saltwater tanks, you'll see the advantages to greater water movement.)

Part I – Designing Your Aquarium Habitat

Estimated Cost:
$100-$500 / £63.71-£318.58

Salt

This is, obviously, an ongoing expense. Five gallons (18.92 liters) of salt will make approximately 150 gallons (567.81 liters) of saltwater.

(Note, you always mix the water outside the tank and add it. Remember, you can add more salt in, but once it's in the water, you can't take it out.)

Estimated Cost:
$50-$75 / £31.85-£47.78

Reverse Osmosis De-Ionization

The Reverse Osmosis De-Ionization (RODI) unit purifies the water for use in a saltwater tank with a degree of efficiency well above any de-chlorination product.

The unit neutralizes the chlorine in tap water while also removing nitrates and phosphates (among other impurities) that are present due to fertilizers, pesticides, and even pharmaceuticals in groundwater.

If fertilizing elements are not removed, the water will promote excess algae growth. Algae are especially problematic if there are too many nutrients in the water, because the lights used in marine tanks are very bright.

Part I – Designing Your Aquarium Habitat

Obviously the other potential contaminants are unhealthy for fish, even if they are — somewhat dubiously — considered safe for human consumption.

Exceptionally pure water is also necessary for the cultivation of coral, and for the health of any invertebrates in your aquarium.

RODI takes place across a five-step filtration sequence:

- The sediment filter removes large impurities like dirt and rust.

- Two carbon blocks take all traces of chlorine out of the water.

- The RO membrane rejects 96-98% of the total dissolved solids present in the water.

- The DI cartridge injects positively and negatively charged ions into the water

The final result is 0 TDS water, which will show no detectable electric charge on a TDS meter. If there were still impurities in the water, electrical conductivity would be evident.

Estimated Cost:
$150-$250 / £95.57-£159.29

Part I – Designing Your Aquarium Habitat

Lighting

Proper lighting is a major element of aesthetic tank design and a matter of considerable debate and opinion. The older style 50/50 bulbs with an actinic element create a desirable "blue" appearance to the water, but the newer LED lights are more energy efficient, produce less heat, and add "shimmer."

Since there is no real "right" answer, (unless you're raising coral) your best bet is to look at tanks with different kinds of light and decide which you like best and which fits your budget.

Due to the potential price range, you should budget a great deal more for lighting than you might expect.

Estimated Cost:
$250-$500 / £159.29-£318.69

Substrate and Rock

Micro and macroscopic organisms inhabit "live" rock, which may be one of several types. Assuming that you are starting with a "fish only" aquarium, live rock will not be an issue, but you should understand the term. It's quite common for saltwater hobbyists to progress to keeping a reef tank.

Part I – Designing Your Aquarium Habitat

- coral

Pieces of coral or coral rock that have broken off the edges of reefs and are encrusted with such things as coralline algae and sponges.

- inshore rock

Rock taken from inside a reef that is much more densely covered in organisms like shrimp, crab, mussels, and macroalgae (seaweed).

- dead base rock

Rock that has no population of living organisms and that is used to serve as a base on which to place and arrange living rock. Over time, the living rock will seed the base rock.

Lionfish

Part I – Designing Your Aquarium Habitat

Typically fine sand is used to cover the bottom of a tank. In fish only tanks, it's common to use base rock and some combination of artificial coral to create the desired natural look.

Estimated Cost:
(live rock) 25 lbs. (11.33 kg) $75-$100 / £47.78-£63.74

dry sand (varies by type and color)
approximately $37 / £58 per 30 lbs. / 13.6 kg

Heaters and Chillers

In order to maintain the correct temperature in your tank, you may need a heater, a chiller, or both. Much of this decision lies in where the tank is located in your home or office and how much you can control the climate of the building.

Insulating your tank can improve your ability to regulate temperature, and is also a more energy efficient strategy in terms of required electricity. Both heaters and chillers do use a fair amount of power.

Estimate cost:
heater $200 / $128
chiller $500 / £319

(Note that while there may be some areas of your equipment choice where you can cut a few corners, climate

Part I – Designing Your Aquarium Habitat

control is not one of them. It is essential that you maintain a stable temperature in your saltwater aquarium.)

As a standard rule, the more water in your tank, the more heat it will retain. Just think about how long a bath tub full of water will stay hot, as opposed to how quickly a cup of coffee cools.

Of the two units, an aquarium cooler will have to work the hardest, so if cooling is your primary climate control need, put the greater part of your budget there.

Equipment to Monitor Water Quality

Although it's not necessary to be a chemist to maintain water quality in a marine tank, you will be testing the water regularly. The primary tool you will use to measure salinity is called a refractometer.

Estimated cost:
$150 / £96

You will also need chemical testing kits for such variables as ammonia, phosphates, and nitrates among others.

Estimated cost:
$20-$40 / £12.75-£25.51 per kit

As an alternative to this approach, however, more and more aquarists are opting to monitor their tank with computer-based sensors that not only measure the required

Part I – Designing Your Aquarium Habitat

levels, but also keep a running record of the health of the tank.

The beauty of this approach is that the software can even predict an adverse event before it occurs. Considering the high cost of many saltwater fish and other life forms, the software and sensing system can pay for themselves in short order.

If you can afford this approach, you will automatically cut down your tank maintenance time, and will even have the luxury of checking on your system at a distance via your smartphone.

Foxface Lo

Part I – Designing Your Aquarium Habitat

You can precisely monitor such variables as pH, temperature, salinity, and water level and flow among a host of others. The sensor systems are expandable, and growing rapidly in sophistication.

If you are interested in computerized water monitoring, look at the controllers offered at DigitalAquatics.com. Expect to require a custom quote to get an accurate price.

Estimated Cost:
$500-$1000 / £319-£368

Sump

Essentially a sump is a second tank that is linked to the main tank. Its purpose is to hold a reserve pool of pre-conditioned water.

This is not a necessity, but many aquarists argue that by doubling the total water volume in the tank environment, you will be able to run a healthier aquarium with better water flow and filtration.

Commonly the sump will be designed to sit hidden beneath the main display tank along with other necessary parts of the tank's mechanical systems. Prices will vary by size and water capacity.

Estimated cost:
$280 / £179

Part I – Designing Your Aquarium Habitat

Auto Top Off

This system is designed to maintain the water level in the tank with fresh water when evaporation drops the level to a predetermined point. The design is fairly basic.
A float lowers with the water level and triggers a pump when the set point is reached. Then the water rises, a second trigger shuts the pump off.
Estimated cost:
$175 / £112

Backup Generator

While a backup generator is not a necessity, having one does make sense when you add up your total investment in a saltwater tank in terms of both equipment and livestock.

Tang

Part I – Designing Your Aquarium Habitat

One power failure, and all your work — not to mention the lives of your fish — are snuffed out in just a few hours.

Estimated cost:
7500 watt stand-by generator
$700-$1000 / £447-£638

Overflow Box

An overflow box also belongs in the category of "precautionary equipment." If something goes wrong and an excess of water is pumped into your tank, the overflow box would prevent water damage to the adjacent area.

Estimated cost:
$150 / £96

Installing Tank Components

While there is no one way to set up a saltwater tank — or any aquarium for that matter — the typical sequence runs along these lines.

- Select and purchase a tank in terms of size and material.

- Determine the location of the tank and how it will be supported. (Stand, reinforced flooring, or concrete.)

- Connect the RODI system to ensure water quality from the beginning.

Part I – Designing Your Aquarium Habitat

- If you are planning to use a sump, install that tank and ensure the quality and consistency of the water it will hold.

- Mount the protein skimmer, auto top off system, and heater / chiller as applicable.

- Lay down the substrate and position any rock, live or artificial, along with additional aquarium structures and decorations.

- Mount the powerheads or pumps.

- Fill the tank with premixed saltwater but do NOT add fish.

It is absolutely essential that the water in your aquarium be "cycled" before any fish are introduced. This is a time consuming process, but vital to sustain marine life.

Be prepared for the fact that your new tank may well sit empty for a period of 6-8 weeks before you can begin to introduce fish.

Understanding Basic Water Chemistry

Like any hobby, aquarists have their own "lingo" and their own pet topics. When groups of saltwater enthusiasts gather, water quality is a source of almost endless debate and analysis. This is not, however, a topic to be taken lightly.

Part I – Designing Your Aquarium Habitat

Maintaining good water in your tank means you are responsible for the very atmosphere your fish breathe. The fastest way to kill an entire tank is to ignore their water until it becomes nothing more than a toxic ammonia soup.

The essential measurements with which you will become conversant include:

- pH (power of hydrogen)

An expression of the acidity of water measured on a scale, with ph 5 being slightly acidic and pH 8 alkaline. The neutral position is pH 7. Saltwater has a pH range of 7.5 to 8.4.

- KH (carbonate hardness)

This is not a measure of alkalinity, but rather a measure of how alkaline the water is, meaning, how well will it serve as a buffer to neutralize acid. The higher the KH, the more stable the chemical composition of the water.

- sg (specific gravity)

This reading shows the relative salinity of the water, which is measured with a hydrometer or refractometer. Natural seawater varies in salinity by location from 1.020 to 1.030. Saltwater tank enthusiasts generally strive for a reading of 1.022.

Part I – Designing Your Aquarium Habitat

Water Parameters by Tank Type

The basic parameters that are applicable to each type of tank (along with more advanced readings) are:

specific gravity or salinity:
1.020-1.025 for FO and FOWLR, 1.023-1.025 for reef

temperature:
72-78 F for all

pH:
8.1-8.4 for all

alkalinity:
8-12 dKH for all

ammonia:
undetectable

nitrate:
undetectable.

nitrate - nitrogen:
less than 30.0 ppm for FO and FOWLR, less than 1.0 ppm for reef

phosphate:
less than 1.0 ppm for FO and FOWLR, less than 0.2 ppm for reef

Part I – Designing Your Aquarium Habitat

calcium:
350-450 ppm for all

magnesium:
1150-1350 ppm for FO and FOWLR, 1250-1350 for reef

iodine:
0.04-0.10 ppm for FO and FOWLR, 0.06-0.10 ppm for reef

strontium:

4-10 ppm for FO and FOWLR, 8-14 ppm for reef
You will come to know these and other water quality measurements by heart. In the beginning, however, your primary concern is to be certain that the nitrogen cycle is in place in your tank.

Part I – Designing Your Aquarium Habitat

Cycling Your Tank

Cycling the tank creates an active process that addresses the amount of ammonia that builds up in the water from the waste material produced by fish in a closed environment.

Ammonia becomes toxic to all the life forms in the tank very quickly. If the correct beneficial bacteria are in place to eat the ammonia, it is converted to nitrite, which is, in turn, eaten by more bacteria and changed to harmless nitrate.

This bacteriological food chain is part of your water quality management routine, and can be established in a number of ways:

- By introducing chemicals to the water.

- By introducing a source of ammonia.

- By using "starter fish" that are, in essence, sacrificial lambs.

- By using live rock.

In the shorthand of the aquarium world, this process boils down to "with fish" and "without fish."

The traditional way is to use starter fish, and to hope they survive. Damselfish are typically chosen to cycle a tank because they can withstand the toxic levels of ammonia to which they will be exposed with a fair amount of success.

Part I – Designing Your Aquarium Habitat

Many aquarists, however, balk at what seems like blatant cruelty.

If the "without fish" method is chosen, ammonia must be introduced to the tank in some form, either by chemically adding it to the water, or by putting decomposing matter or fish waste in the aquarium.

The purpose is to cultivate the beneficial bacteria that will start to break the ammonia down into nitrites and ultimately nitrates. The goal is to achieve an environment where nitrates are present at a level below 10 parts per million.

When cycling without fish, raise the water temperature to 86F-95F (30C-35C) until the water stabilizes, then slowly cool it back down to a range of 74F-80F (23.3C-26.6C). You do not want to stress and kill the bacteria you have just cultivated with a rapid shift in temperature.

Estimated Setup Costs

Aquarium
180 gallon / 681.37 liter tank $350 / £223

Protein Skimmer
$350 / £223

Pumps or Powerheads
$100-$500 / £63.71-£318.58

Part I – Designing Your Aquarium Habitat

Salt
$50-$75 / £31.85-£47.78

Reverse Osmosis De-Ionization (RODI) Unit
$150-$250 / £95.57-£159.29

Lighting
$250-$500 / £159.29-£318.69

Substrate and Sand
(live rock) 25 lbs. (11.33 kg) $75-$100 / £47.78-£63.74

dry sand (varies by type and color)
approximately $37 / £58 per 30 lbs. / 13.6 kg

Temperature Control
heater $200 / $128
chiller $500 / £319

Refractometer
$150 / £96

Water testing kits
$20-$40 / £12.75-£25.51 per kit

Computer-based water monitoring (optional)
$500-$1000 / £319-£368

Sump
$280 / £179

Part I – Designing Your Aquarium Habitat

Auto Top Off
$175 / £112

Backup Generator (optional)
7500 watt stand-by
$700-$1000 / £447-£638

Overflow Box
$150 / £96

Sample Beginner Fish

8 Blue/Green Chromis
$320.00/£200.00

2 Lemon Butterflyfish
$60.00/£38.00

1 Coral Beauty Angelfish
$22.00/£14.00

1 Pacific Blue Tang
$30.00/£19.00

1 Clownfish
$25.00/£6.00

You can set up your saltwater tank for:

Part I – Designing Your Aquarium Habitat

Minimum Requirements
$4494.00/£2827.00

Maximum Requirements
$6114.00/£3845.00

Part I – Designing Your Aquarium Habitat

Part II – Populating Your Saltwater Tank

Many beginning aquarists take the "kid in a candy store" approach to populating their tanks. This is a serious mistake for many reasons.

You will likely buy too many fish and not pay proper attention to population management in terms of compatibility.

Rather than simply going to an aquarium store and "window shopping," it's best to plan your tank population in advance. Err on the side of less is more, and make sure the mix of fish you're considering can cohabitate peacefully.

Things to Consider Before You Buy

There are many theories about minimizing aggression and territoriality in a tank. Of these, maintaining a good mix of fish from different families can go a long way toward keeping the peace. Aggression in fish is typically directed toward their own kind.

This response may be purely instinct on the part of the fish. They know what they like to eat, so by attacking their relatives who want to eat the same things, the fish is simply protecting what he sees as a limited food supply. This holds true even in an environment where ample food is provided.

Part II – Populating Your Saltwater Tank

Butterfly Fish

It's also important to consider the vertical and horizontal spaces in the tank and to select species that occupy different niches and zones.

Obviously if you overstock a particular region of this enclosed environment, you're setting the stage for an underwater turf war.

It's always a mistake to just go for the "pretty" fish, or the ones you find attractive for other reasons. Population management has to be based on a complete understanding of how any one fish will live and behave in the tank.

For beginners, stick to the one inch (2.54 cm) of fish per 5 gallons (18.9 liters) of water rule.

Part II – Populating Your Saltwater Tank

Terms Used to Describe Fish

You will run across a wide variety of terms and phrases used to describe fish. Some of these include, but are not limited to:

peaceful - Basically, these fish play well with others, and are not bothersome to other tank mates.

spirited - This does not mean aggressive, only that they fish in question are lively and may chase, but not eat or attack tankmates.

mildly aggressive - These fish have the potential to be bullies and should not be housed with species that are markedly timid or slow.

aggressive - These fish should only be kept with fish of equal or larger size that are active and basically able to defend themselves.

territorial - Fish that stake a claim to a portion of the tank, whether that be a level of the water, or a decorative structure, which they claim as their own are said to be territorial. Their defensive reaction may be limited to chasing off other fish, or to actually attacking them.

changeable - Changeable fish may start out peaceful, or even timid, but become more aggressive as they get older and bigger. Some will even start to eat smaller fish.

Part II – Populating Your Saltwater Tank

fast growth - These are fish that will not only grow quickly, but will likely get much larger than their size at purchase. Never get a fast growth fish without finding out their maximum size at maturity.

carnivorous - Fish that eat only meat — including other fish.

herbivorous - Fish that eat only plant or vegetable matter.

eats sessile invertebrates - These fish will consume live coral, sponges, feather dusters, anemones, and live rocks.

eats motile invertebrates - These fish will consume starfish, shrimp, and crabs.

filter feeder - This is a fish that may require liquified food.

Any time you are considering purchasing a fish or other living creature that is described in a way you do not understand, do your homework before you introduce the specimen to your tank.

Population management is one of the most challenging aspects of keeping a marine aquarium.

You must consider every living thing that goes into your tank not just in terms of its individual requirements, but how it will fit into the closed environment you are cultivating.

Part II – Populating Your Saltwater Tank

Yellow Tang

Buying Healthy Fish

In selecting fish, it's important to recognize any signs of bad health or stress. These include:

- A cloudy appearance to the eyes.

- Any fins that are frayed, tattered, torn, or damaged.

- Lacerations on the body or any visible red streaks.

- A salt-like substance adhering to the body or eyes, which is an indicator of parasites.

- Any cotton-like growths on the body indicating the presence of fungus.

Part II – Populating Your Saltwater Tank

Any fish you purchase should be responsive and active, not constantly hiding in the tank or remaining completely motionless. Ask to see the fish eat before buying it and taking it home.

Best Fish Lists?

Go on any search engine and you'll find a proliferation of "best" lists for all kinds of suggested tank populations. Any group of fish that successfully live together is, by anyone's definition, a "best" case scenario. Take any list of this type as a starting point for populating your tank.

For Beginners

The species here are chosen for their moderate care requirements and semi-aggressive behavior. All are omnivores or carnivores, so their dietary needs are simple. They are more tolerant of changes in water chemistry and fairly disease resistant. All will work well in 10-30 gallon (38-114 liter) tanks and up.

Damselfish

Damselfish are brightly colored, active and hardy, ranging in size from 2"-5" (5 – 12.7 cm) depending on the species. As a close relative of the clown fish, they are often most colorful as juveniles and less vibrant as adults.

They do have a tendency to be highly territorial toward their own kind, a trait that gets worse with age. Most

Part II – Populating Your Saltwater Tank

damselfish will live five years or more with proper care. They are omnivores and do well on flaked, pellet, frozen or live food sources.
Estimated Cost: $5 - 10

Clownfish

Clownfish also live five years are more and are of an equal size with damselfish in the 2"-5"+ (5 – 12.7 cm) range. They do best when kept with a companion anemone, since these bright, hardly little creatures shelter within the anemone's stinging tentacles.

Like damselfish, clownfish are omnivores and will happily eat flaked, pellet, frozen or live food.
Estimated Cost: $15 - 30

Blue Green Chromis

A type of damselfish, Blue Green Chromis reach an adult size of as much as 3" (7.62 cm). They are schooling fish with a very peaceful disposition and a lovely green color that seems to shimmer as they swim.

Like all damselfish, Blue Green Chromis are omnivores.
Estimated Cost: $5

Firefish

The Firefish (or Firefish Goby or Firefish Dartfish) is a timid, but sweet-tempered fish that likes to stay in small

Part II – Populating Your Saltwater Tank

schools. They are brilliantly colored with bright yellow heads that progress through a light, pinkish body to a vibrant red tail. The fins are strikingly jet black.

With their torpedo-like bodies that reach a length of 1.5"-3.5" (3.81 - 8.89 cm).

Firefish look like they could be aggressive, but they do best in peaceful tanks. They are jumpers, however, so a lid is highly recommended. As carnivores, they require live or dead animal-based foods.

Estimated Cost: $10

Kaudern's Cardinal Fish

Also known as the Banggai Cardinal Fish or the Long-Finned Cardinal Fish, this semi-aggressive fish is hard to miss in a tank. A flashing silver highlighted by bold black stripes and white body spots, their long elegant fins flow beautifully as they swim.

As carnivores that reach about 3" (7.62 cm) in length, Kaudern's Cardinals need a well-balanced, meaty diet of items like feeder shrimp and bloodworms. Larger specimens will enjoy feeder fish.

Estimated Cost: $25

For Fish Only Tanks

As your saltwater aquarium grows in complexity with your level of experience, you can begin to populate the tank (as

Part II – Populating Your Saltwater Tank

room allows) with species that occupy different vertical and horizontal spaces in the environment.

Some aggressive fish can live together, since they don't venture into each other's tank level. You have to be careful however, if you mix peaceful bottom dwellers with a benthic omnivore, the results can be disastrous — and costly.

Moving to a fish only aquarium with more complex issues of tank management is, however, the next logical progression in the development of your marine hobby. It will also further illustrate how important it is to carefully plan the parameters of your population for maximum success.

Eels

There are approximately 20 species of eels from which to choose. Three examples include the Snowflake eel (pictured below), the Ghost eel, and the Chain eel.

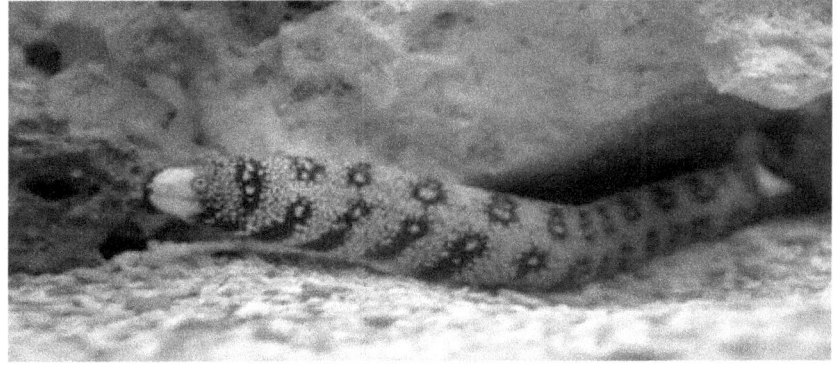

Part II – Populating Your Saltwater Tank

All eels are snakelike in appearance and have "whiskers" or barbels protruding from their faces. At purchase, most specimens are one-third to one-half their ultimate adult size. Be prepared for these creatures to get bigger!

The Snowflake eel (also called the Snowflake Moray eel, Clouded Moray, or Starry Moray) is semi-aggressive. A beautiful blend of black, tan, and white, Snowflakes are gorgeous, but they are escape artists, so a lid is a must.

Since this carnivorous creature reaches a maximum size of 2' (60.96 cm), be careful not to mix them with fish that are small enough to be swallowed.

Snowflakes sell at an opening price of $22 (£13.84).

Ghost eels, by comparison, can reach a maximum length of 3'4" (101.6 cm). Their bodies are primarily white, with black spots on the head and face. The colors may darken as they age. They are also carnivores and are considered semi-aggressive.

Ghost eels start at $40 (£25.16) each.

Chain eels can grow to an adult length of 2'4" (71.12 cm). They have a white, yellowish body with "chain" markings in black, brown, or gray. Also called the Chainlink Moray Eel, it needs to be able to find refuge between coral and rock so it can hide by day and search for food at night. They are semi-aggressive carnivores.

Part II – Populating Your Saltwater Tank

Expect to pay $50 (£31.45) per eel.

Please note that within this group, some more exotic specimens can cost in excess of $400 (£251.62). When shopping for eels, budget accordingly.

Red Grouper Fish

Groupers

There are approximately 17 different groupers from which aquarists may choose. Three examples are the Miniatus Grouper, the Red Flag Grouper, and the Spotted Grouper. All are aggressive carnivores that eat meaty foods. Purchase sizes on groupers can be as little as 2" (5.08 cm) but be prepared — these fish grow!

The Miniatus Grouper (also known as the Miniata Grouper, Coral, Blue Spot Rock Cod, Coral Hind, or Coral Grouper)

Part II – Populating Your Saltwater Tank

is a spectacular fish. He'll look fantastic in your tank, but don't trust him with anything small enough to swallow, including invertebrates.

With a gorgeous orange body, and yellow fins and tail — all spotted in vibrant blue, this big handsome fish generally grows to no more than 1' (2.54 cm) in captivity, but can reach 18" (45.72 cm)in the wild.

The estimated cost for a Miniatus Grouper is $60 (£38) and up.

The Red Flag Grouper (Flag Tailed Grouper, Darkfinned Hind, Banded-Tail Coral-Cod, or V-Tailed Grouper) is solid red, darkening toward the caudal fin with some white markings and a distinctive white "v" on the tail. They reach a maximum length of 11" (27.94 cm).

Red Flag Groupers start at $30 (£19).

The Spotted Grouper (White Spotted Grouper Summan Grouper, or Speckled Fin Grouper) sports white polka dots on a brown to black body. They reach a maximum size of one foot.

As an opening price, expect to pay $19 (£12).

Soldierfish

The Popeye Catalufa Soldierfish (Bigeye Soldierfish) is a peaceful carnivore, but it will eat invertebrates.

Part II – Populating Your Saltwater Tank

Black Bar Soldier Fish

This nocturnal fish hides when the lights are on, but when you get a glimpse of it, you'll be treated to the sight of a vibrant burned orange to red specimen with white highlights. The dorsal fin is feathery, and all fins are black tipped. They grow to a maximum length of 7 inches (17.78 cm).

The approximate starting cost for this fish is $100 (£63).

The Big Eye Black Bar Soldierfish, also a peaceful meat-eater, reaches a maximum size of 8 inches (20.32 cm).

Alternately called the Blackbar Soldierfish, it is bright red with thin white outlining on the fins. With its unusually large eyes, this specimen will stand out in your tank. Prices start at $15 (£9).

Puffers

Puffers represent a grouping of fish with more than 25 members typically kept by enthusiasts.

The tan and yellow Spiny Box Puffer (Web Burr Fish) sports both dark spots and short, fixed spines that serve as protection. The teeth are fused into a beak-like structure making this a truly unique fish in terms of appearance. A semi-aggressive carnivore, it will grow to a length of 10" (25.4 cm) and sells for an opening price of $25 (£16).

The Stars and Stripes Puffer, also a semi-aggressive carnivore, will reach a maximum size of 1'6" (46 cm).

Puffer Fish

Part II – Populating Your Saltwater Tank

This ornate fish is covered with white spots on the upper half set against a greenish tan. On the lower half, there are striking horizontal stripes. The fins are darker at the base, rounding out the distinctive overall look. The average starting price is $40 (£25).

Porcupine Puffer, like its fellows, is semi-aggressive, but is an omnivore that reaches a length of one foot. Also called simply the Porcupine Fish, this creature's gray to tannish body is covered in spines, and it lacks pelvic fins. Expect to pay $30 (£19).

Lionfish

There are nine varieties of Lionfish.

The semi-aggressive Dwarf / Zebra Lionfish grows to a maximum length of 7 inches (17.78 cm). It is venomous and is a carnivore.

Marked with red, white, and black vertical stripes along the body, the pectoral fins are large and fan like. The quill-shaped dorsal fins are tall and carry the creature's venom. The stings are akin to that of a bee. The opening price is $20 (£13).

Russell's Lionfish grows to a length of 1'2" (35.56 cm) and displays the same semi-aggressive behavior. A fish of many names, it is alternately identified as the Red Volitans, the Spotless or Soldier Lionfish, the Large Tail or Military

Part II – Populating Your Saltwater Tank

Turkey Fish and the Plain Tail Firefish. The coloration is tan with light-brown vertical stripes.

The dorsal, anal, and pectoral spines are fleshy and do not display the banding typical of other lionfish. These spines are poisonous and again deliver a bee-like sting. It is peaceful except toward other lionfish, and has a hardy constitution. Expect to pay $30 (£19) and up.

The Fu Manchu Lionfish reaches a size of only 4". A semi-aggressive, venomous, carnivore its alternate names are Twin Spot Lionfish or Ocellated Lionfish.

It has red, white, and black vertical striping on the body, fan-like pectorals, and tall, quill-like, stinging dorsals. There are two feeler-like appendages on the chin not seen in other lionfish. The average purchase price is $30 (£19).

Larger Angels

There are 36 species of Angel Fish, all popular with aquarists for their wide range of colors from black and yellow to blue, orange, and white.

The Blueline Angel Fish (Bluebanded Angel Fish) is a semi-aggressive omnivore that will reach a maximum length of 8 inches (20.32 cm) and requires a minimum tank size of 180 gallons (681.37 liter).

Juveniles have black bodies with iridescent blue horizontal stripes and a yellow vertical bar behind the eye. Both the

Part II – Populating Your Saltwater Tank

dorsal and anal fins are outlined in white, while the caudal fin is bright yellow. In adults, the bodies lighten to yellow or tan.

These fish are shy when first introduced to a tank, but adapt quickly and do well with non-aggressive tank mates. Blueline Angels do enjoy lots of good hiding places. Prices start at $200 (£126).

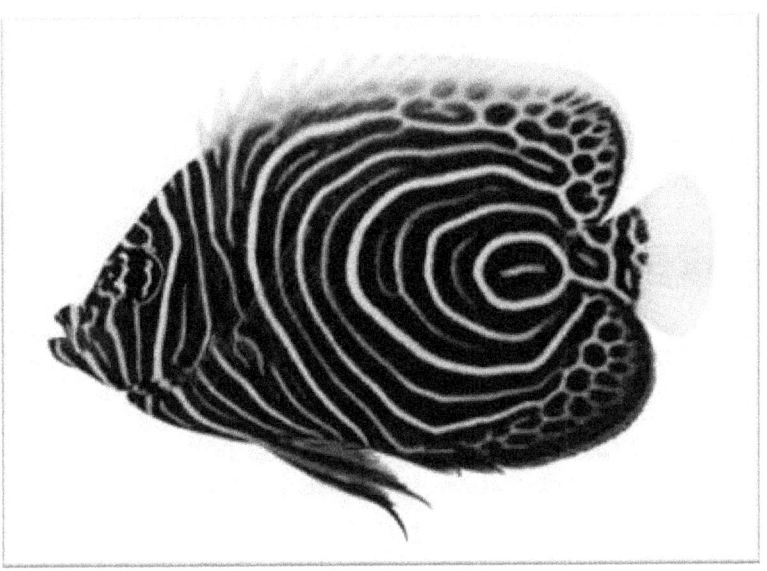

Emperor Angelfish

The Fireball Angel Fish (Flameback Pygmy Angel Fish or Flameback Angel Fish or Brazilian Flameback Angel Fish) is often confused with the African Flameback Angel Fish.

The Fireball is a semi-aggressive omnivore that will reach a maximum size of 3 inches (7.62 cm). They have a distinctive dark blue caudal fine, while the body is brilliant to dark blue with a dorsal swatch of orange.

Part II – Populating Your Saltwater Tank

This fish can damage a reef system since it will nip at corals. Tanks with multiple hiding places are recommended. Fireballs sell for $80 (£50) and up.

The Singapore Angel Fish (Vermiculated Angel Fish) is a semi-aggressive omnivore that reaches a maximum size of 7 inches (17.78 cm). They have blue lips and a yellow nose with a black, vertical band over the eyes to create the look of a mask.

A band of yellow borders the mask followed by a wider white band. The body is primarily black, while the dorsal and anal fins are outlined in sapphire blue. The caudal fin is yellow or gray.

Singapore Angels can be challenging to keep. Not all specimens acclimate well, with some individuals being prone to hiding constantly and refusing food. The species as a whole does better in a quiet tank with a non-aggressive population.

Provide plenty of hiding places, and be aware that this fish will nip at corals and seaweed. Prices start at $24 (£15).

Butterfly Fish

There are 36 varieties of Butterfly Fish. All are peaceful carnivores or omnivores.

The Copperband Butterfly Fish (Beaked Butterfly Fish, Beaked Coral Fish, Orange Striped Butterfly) is a peaceful

Part II – Populating Your Saltwater Tank

carnivore that grows to a maximum 8 inches (20.32 cm). It uses its long, narrow nose and mouth to hunt in crevices and holes. The markings of this species include yellow-orange vertical bands edged in black. The rear of the dorsal fin is marked with a false eye spot.

These fish do best singularly in peaceful tanks with no similar butterfly fish. They may pick at anemones and feather dusters, and are shy, deliberate feeds. On average the Copperband Butterfly fish sells for $27 (£17).

The Lemon Butterfly Fish (Milletseed Butterfly Fish or Millet Butterfly Fish) is also a peaceful carnivore, but only reaches 5 inches (12.7 cm) in length.

This variety is primarily yellow, but is marked with multiple dark spots that form vertical stripes on the body. There is a black bar through the eyes, and the fins are yellow.

This is an excellent fish for a beginner. They need lots of room to swim, and thrive in peaceful community tanks when kept singly or as part of a pair introduced to the aquarium at the same time. You will pay about $30 (£19) per fish. The Lemon Butterfly fish is a carnivore.

The Dusky Butterfly Fish (Black Butterfly Fish or Orange Nosed Butterfly) is a peaceful omnivore that grows no larger than 8 inches (20.32 cm). It is marked with a contrasting set of golden orange and yellow rings that encircle a disc-shaped purple-black body.

Part II – Populating Your Saltwater Tank

In mature specimens the snout-like mouth turns white with a yellow band, while the body darkens. The species also has a characteristic lump on the forehead. Prices for the Dusky Butterfly Fish start at $120 (£75).

Largers Wrasses

There are 80 species or larger Wrasses, the bulk of which are peaceful to semi-aggressive carnivores.

The Cuban Hogfish (Spotfin Hogfish) is a semi-aggressive carnivore with a pinkish orange head and body that becomes more yellow toward the tail. The placement and hue of the colors varies widely by individual, however.

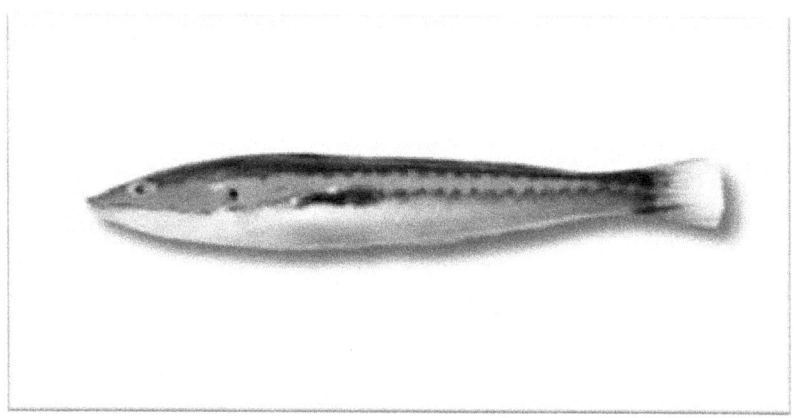

Rainbow Wrasse

At a length of 8 inches (20.32 cm), the Cuban Hogfish needs plenty of room to swim, but is an excellent choice for a beginner with a large tank due to its generally docile nature.

Part II – Populating Your Saltwater Tank

The Cuban Hogfish should only be housed with larger tank mates, however, since it can be a bit of a bully at feeding time. Prices for this species begin at $100 (£63).

The Green Wrasse is also an 8-inch (20.32 cm) carnivore, but is even more peaceful. You will also see this fish referred to as the Pastel Green Wrasse or the Green Coris. It has no extravagant markings, but is lovely in its simplicity.

A tight fitting lid is recommended since Green Wrasses are jumpers. They will also hide in the sand at the bottom of the tank when frightened. Prices for this species begin at $17 (£11).

The semi-aggressive Mystery Wrasse (White Barred Wrasse or Five Barred Wrasse) is a carnivore that grows no larger than 4.75 inches (12.06 cm). The yellow, blue and purple hues seem to outline a smile on the face, making this fish stand out in any tank.

The body is red to maroon and marked with thin, vertical white stripes. A yellow hue surrounds the false eye spot on the green tail. Younger individuals will more green on the body, but this disappears quickly.

A somewhat difficult species to locate, they are popular in reef tanks due to their placid nature, but they will constantly search for food in the form of small crustaceans. Mystery Wrasses need lots of live rock in which to hide and prefer a sandy bottom for the same reason. The average cost is $100 (£63).

Part II – Populating Your Saltwater Tank

Trigger Fish

There are approximately 50 varieties of Trigger Fish, but many require 300 gallon (1135.62 liter) tanks and more.

The Red Tail Trigger Fish (Sargassum Trigger Fish) is one of the smaller specimens, reaching a maximum length of 10 inches (25.4 cm). Mostly purple in color, its sides are marked with darker, evenly spaced spots.

Overall, the body of this aggressive carnivore is outlined in darker lines that progress toward the red tail, from which the species draws its name.

A Red Tail Trigger Fish will rearrange landscaping and rocks in a tank as it wanders around looking for food. The species also has a grunting vocalization and is unusually friendly. Prices start at $120 (£75).

Parrot Fish

The Parrot Fish is also seen listed as the Bluehead Fairy Wrasse, Bluescaled Fairy Wrasse, Yellow Flanked Fairy Wrasse, Purplehead Parrot Wrasse, or the Blue-Sided Fairy Wrasse. It is a peaceful carnivore that grows no larger than 5 inches (12.7 cm).

Colors will range from red and blue to deep maroon and blue, but the underside is typically pale. These fish are ideal for reef tanks due to their bright coloration and engaged level of activity. Expect to pay $30 (£19) per fish.

Part II – Populating Your Saltwater Tank

Tangs

There are 47 varieties of tangs, most being semi-aggressive herbivores. The Blue Tang (Palette Surgeon Fish, Pacific Blue Tang, Hepatus or Regal Tang) grows to a length of 12" (2.54 cm) and is distinctive for its electric blue body and bold, black markings.

Blue Tang

The black, which begins at the eye, traces the dorsal line back toward the tail, where it turns to move forword above the pectoral fin, creating a shape like that of a painter's palette.

The Blue Tang is normally peaceful, but will be aggressive toward its own kind. If multiple specimens are kept, they

Part II – Populating Your Saltwater Tank

should be introduced at the same time in a large community tank.

Blue Tangs are active swimmers, but they also love to hide in live rock. The recommended minimum tank size for this species is 180 gallons. Also, watch them carefully. The species is unusually susceptible to lateral line disease, fin erosion, ich, and skin parasites.

On average, expect to pay $30 (£19) for a Blue Tang.

The slightly smaller Powder Blue Tang can be housed in 125 gallon tank and reaches a maximum length of 9 inches (22.86 cm). You will also see this species called the Powder Blue Surgeon Fish.

Their oval bodies have bold, colorful markings in varying shades of blue, with bright yellow highlights on the dorsal and pectoral fins. Both the face and tail are outlined in a striking blue black.

These fish are very aggressive toward other Tangs and Surgeon Fish and should be kept alone unless placed in unusually large tanks. You will pay about $60 (£38) per fish for this species.

Surgeon Fish

There are 8 varieties of surgeon fish, which are semi-aggressive herbivores. The Chevron Tang (Hawaiian

Part II – Populating Your Saltwater Tank

Bristletooth, Hawaiian Surgeon Fish, Black Surgeon Fish) reaches a maximum size of 11 inches (27.94 cm).

Their oval bodies have radiating, bold markings that change as the fish ages. Juveniles are bright orange with violet patterns on the body and fins, while in mature specimens the pattern becomes olive brown.

While peaceful with most other fish, the Chevron Tang will be aggressive with other Tangs. Expect to pay $200 (£126) and up for this striking fish.

The Convict Tang or Convict Surgeon Fish (pictured above) is equally distinctive with its white to silver body marked with six vertical, black bars. It reaches a maximum size of 8 inches.

It should not be housed with other Tangs, but will live peacefully with other Convict Tangs if they are introduced to the tank at the same time.

This is a difficult species to breed in captivity since the fry remain in the planktonic stage for months and are easily killed by tank filters. You will pay approximately $27 (£17) for a Convict Tang.

Rabbit Fish

Rabbit Fish

Rabbit Fish are peaceful herbivores. The Yellowblotch Rabbit Fish (also known as the Orange Spotted Spine Foot,

Part II – Populating Your Saltwater Tank

Orange Spotted Fox-Face Rabbit Fish, or Gold Saddle Rabbit Fish) reaches a maximum size of 1'4" (40.64 cm). This fish is increasingly popular with reef aquarists because it earns its keep eating algae. They are also beautiful additions to any community. The brown body is covered in orange spots, with a yellow posterior false eye.

The dorsal spines are venomous, so this fish must be handled with care. They are peaceful, however, except with other Rabbit Fish.

They can be housed with more aggressive fish, due to the presence of their protective spines. The opening price for the species is $40 (£25).

The One Spot Fox Face is smaller, at a maximum size of 7 inches (17.78 cm). This graceful fish, also called the Blotched Fox Face, has a distinct eye spot on the body. The markings range from symmetrical circles to a free-form patches and are unique by individual.

This species is peaceful until housed with other Rabbit Fish. Expect to pay $30 (£19) and up per fish.

Boxfish

There are 4 varieties of Boxfish. They are semi-aggressive omnivores. The Cubicus Box Fish reaches a maximum size of 1' 6" (45.72 cm). It is also called the Yellow Box Fish, Polka Dot Boxfish, and the Cubed Boxfish.

Part II – Populating Your Saltwater Tank

Boxfish

Juveniles have yellow, box-shaped bodies with brown spots. In adults, the yellow fades to brown. They require, at minimum, a 125 gallon (473.18 liters) aquarium. They are, however, difficult fish to keep.

Not only will they nibble at tubeworms in reef tanks, but if stressed, they release a poisonous ostracitoxin that will quickly kill other fish. The opening price is $20 (£13).

The "plain" Box Fish is also a semi-aggressive omnivore, but smaller at a maximum size of 10 inches (25.4 cm). Also known as the Spotted Box Fish, Blue Box Fish, Black Fox Fish, and White Spotted Box Fish, they release the same poison when stressed.

Part II – Populating Your Saltwater Tank

Males have vibrant blue bodies with a wide black swatch covering the upper portion like a cap.

The spots that cover the body are white on black and black on blue, with thin, horizontal orange stripes on the tail. Females are entirely black with white dots. The opening price for the species is $30 (£19).

Mandarins

The Green Mandarin is a peaceful, four-inch carnivore also called the Striped Mandarin Fish or the Green Mandarin Fish. Popular for its unusual beauty, the Green Mandarin sports a maze of blue, orange, and green markings on the head and body.

Mandarin

Part II – Populating Your Saltwater Tank

Keep this fish in a well-established tank with live rock or live sand. You should be able to purchase Green Mandarins for about $17 (£11).

The Red Mandarin is more expensive at $30 (£19), but is the same size at a maximum of four inches. Also a peaceful carnivore, the maze of markings on this variety are blue, orange, and red, with pronounced stripes and red on the pectoral fins.

Red Mandarins are a rare find, but very popular. They also require live rock and live sand to thrive.

Squirrelfish

Squirrelfish

Part II – Populating Your Saltwater Tank

There are 5 varieties of Squirrelfish. The Striped Squirrelfish is a seven-inch, peaceful, carnivore also called the Hawaiian Squirrel Fish.

The body is bright red with thin, white horizontal stripes. It is nocturnal, and will hide when the lights are on. The opening price is $30 (£19).

The Flashlight Fish, also a peaceful carnivore, grows to no more than 9 inches (22.86 cm). Also called the Twofin Flashlight Fish or Lantern Fish, it has a black body with a bluish hue to the dorsal and caudal fins.

The Flashflight Fish is more distinctive feature is its glowing smile, created by bioluminiscent bacteria present in light organs below each eye. The "light" can be white, blue, or yellow depending on the mood of the fish.

Amazingly, the fish can rotate the light organs in their sockets in "on" and "off" positions. The lights are used for communication, defense, and to attract plankton for food. Needless to say, this $90 (£57) fish makes an unforgettable addition to any aquarium.

Batfish

There are four varieties of Batfish. They grow very quickly and most reach a size of around 15 inches (38.1 cm). A smaller example of the species is the peaceful Long Nose Batfish, a 9.5 inch (24.13 cm) carnivore also called the Walking Batfish.

Part II – Populating Your Saltwater Tank

It has a horizontally flattened body of mottled reddish brown, and sells for $60 (£38).

Blennies

There are 44 varieties. The Bicolor Blennie reaches a maximum size of 4 inches and is a peaceful herbivore. Its anterior half can be blue to dull brown, while the posterior half is dull orange.

Males of this species are larger and go through a succession of color changes, including a switch to blue when breeding. This species will pick on their own kind, smaller gobies, and dartfish. Expect to pay about $17 (£11) per Bicolor Blennie.

The Horned Blennie is also a peaceful plant eater, but will grow no larger than 2.24 inches (5.68 cm). It is mottled tan with darker spots on the body and fins. The most distinctive feature of this fish are its two large branching horns.

The species will display aggression toward tank mates of similar shape, and does best housed singly or as a mated pair.

They exhibit the charming behavior of perching and hopping about on rocks and decorations in search of microalgae, and are thus an interesting addition to a tank at a cost of just $30 (£9) per fish.

Part II – Populating Your Saltwater Tank

Moderate to Advanced Tanks

Many of the fish already discussed are also appropriate for moderate to advanced tanks. These include Surgeons, Triggerfish, Angels, Lionfish, Clownfish, Damselfish, Wrasses, Eels, and Butterflyfish. Others that can be added into the mix include the following.

Basslets

There are 20 varieties of Basslets. These fish are peaceful to semi-aggressive carnivores. The Black Cap Basslet, at 4 inches (10.16 cm) is somewhat aggressive, but really poses a threat to smaller invertebrates only.

Basslet

Part II – Populating Your Saltwater Tank

Black Caps have brilliant purple bodies and a jet black diagonal cap. They like to hide in rock caves and because they are territorial, should not be kept with other basslets.

As deep water bottom dwellers, they prefer to live in tanks with subdued lighting. Expect to pay $70 (£44) and up for this species.

The Gold Assessor Basslet is somewhat smaller at 3 inches. A peaceful carnivore, you will also see this fish listed as the Golden Mini Grouper. It is entirely yellow with red outlining the fins.

Gold Assessors will not bother invertebrates, but the males are aggressive and territorial. The opening price for this species is $100 (£63).

Seahorses

There are several varieties of seahorse that can be housed in saltwater tanks. One of the hardiest and most energetic is the peaceful Black Seahorse, which grows to a maximum size of 6" (15.24 cm). Typically black or yellow, the colors will change to match the creature's mood.

Seahorses are carnivores, preferring small crustaceans like Mysis shrimp. They are social and thrive when kept as mated paris with small, shy fish. Fast moving territorial fish may harass or stress seahorses. The little creatures are not strong swimmers and prefer to hang on to live rock or decorations with their prehensile tails.

Part II – Populating Your Saltwater Tank

If you keep a mated pair, the minimum tank size is 50 gallons (189 liters.) Expect to pay $60 / £38 per seahorse.

Filefish

There are more than 90 species of filefish. Most do not exceed 6 inches (15.24 cm) in length. The Colored Filefish is found in black, orange, and red with a black or gray head.

This peaceful omnivore grows to a maximum size of only 4" (10.16 cm). They may be difficult to feed at first, and should be allowed to eat coral before being given a regular diet of mysis shrimp, squid, scallops, or freeze-dried krill. This fish does have to be fed three times a day.

The average cost is $15 / £9.

The larger and more expensive Tassle Filefish sells for $40-$80 / £25-£50 and reaches a maximum size of 1' (30.48 cm). They have green bodies with dark horizontal stripes. Generally peaceful, this species will show aggression toward its own kind.

Gobies

There are more than 80 species of Goby in a wide range of colors and sizes. The Sleeper Green Banded Goby is a striking fish with an iridescent blue line bordered in black and orange running from the nose backward under the eye stopping in line with the dorsal fin. The body is pewter with olive overtones.

Part II – Populating Your Saltwater Tank

A peaceful carnivore, the Green Banded Goby grows to a length of 5" / 13 cm. A live sand substrate is recommended for this species. Prices start at $25 / £16.

Reef Tanks

Many of the fish already discussed including Tangs, Trigger Fish, Butterflyfish, Clownfish, and Gobies will do well in reef tanks. In many ways, it's almost more important to know what NOT to put in a tank of this sort.

You certainly want to avoid carnivores that will eat smaller fish. These include eels, groupers, soldierfish, puffers, and lionfish.

The larger varieties of angels will eat corals, crabs, and snails or pick at them until they die. Other fish that will exhibit similar behavior include butterfly fish, larger wrasses, triggerfish, and parrot fish.

Invertebrates

There are many choices of invertebrates for saltwater tanks, but these creatures can be "cannon fodder" in a beginning tank. If you don't do a careful job of picking your fish, the invertebrates will essentially serve as snacks.

Some good invertebrates for beginners including the following, but always match them carefully to the fish with which you are populating your tank.

Part II – Populating Your Saltwater Tank

- Banded Coral Shrimp - $9 / £6
- Blue and Pink Sea Star - $20 / £13
- Blue Tuxedo Urchin - $19 / £12
- Bumble Bee Snail - $3 / £2
- Dwarf Colored Feather Duster $9 / £6
- Electric Blue Hermit Crab - $9 / £6

Beginners should look for hardy invertebrates that require little care. Remember, however, that all of these creatures are sensitive to copper.

Coral

Most beginners do not start with a reef tanks. When your interest does begin to evolve in that direction, "beginner" coral assortments are generally offered by marine supply houses in "starter packs" chosen for their compatibility to given water parameters.

As an example of this kind of product an assortment of coral including a mix of Button Polyp, Yellow Colony Polyp, Hairy Mushroom Coral, and Bullseye Mushroom Coral sells for approximately $130 / £81.

Acclimatization Techniques

Why is it necessary to acclimatize new fish in your tank? We always come back to water chemistry. The fish or invertebrates (including coral) that you have purchased are, in essence, coming from a different "ocean."

Part II – Populating Your Saltwater Tank

They are transitioning from an environment with a different temperature, pH, and specific gravity (salinity) than your tank. They have to be acclimatized to survive, much less thrive.

This is not a process that should EVER be rushed. Simply dumping new fish in an existing tank is an often fatal shock to their systems.

First, turn off the lights in your tank for at least four hours to help with the adjustment process.

In the best of all possible worlds, you would be able to quarantine new fish in a separate tank for two weeks to make sure they are not carrying parasites or a disease, and that they are eating properly.

For most aquarists, especially beginners, this is not a practical recommendation, however.

Floating Acclimatization

With this method, you will begin with all the aquarium lights off, and the lights in the room dimmed. Fish should always be transported inside an opaque container and not immediately exposed to bright light, which causes severe stress and trauma.

- Take the sealed bag with the new fish and allow it to float for 15 minutes in your tank so the temperature can equalize.

Part II – Populating Your Saltwater Tank

- Next, cut open the bag just under the clip or fastener. Roll the edges of the bag down about an inch and create an air pocket so the bag will continue to float. If the bag contains heavy coral and won't float, place the bag in a specimen container or plastic bowl.

- Take 1/2 cup (0.42 UK) of water from the tank and gently add it to the water in the bag.

- Every 5 minutes, add another 1/2 cup (0.42 liters) of water until the bag is full.

- Five minutes after the bag is full, lift it from the tank and discard half of the water it contains.

- Float the bag again and repeat the addition of 1/2 cup (0.42 liters) water every five minutes until it is full again.

At this point, you can gently net the fish or other creature and release it into the tank. Discard the bag. DO NOT pour the water from the bag into your tank at any time.

Drip Acclimatization

This method is more time consuming, and is considered appropriate for the introduction of more sensitive tank inhabitants like coral, shrimp, sea stars, and wrasses.

You will have to actively monitor the drip method, and will need a segment of airline tubing and a 3-5 gallon (11.35-18.92 liter) bucket.

Part II – Populating Your Saltwater Tank

Begin this procedure with the same three steps of the floating method.

- Turn off the lights in the tank.

- Remove the bag with the fish or life form in a dim room.

- Float the sealed bag in your aquarium for 15 minutes.

Once the temperature in the bag has equalized with that of the water in your tank, carefully empty the water and the invertebrate it contains into the bucket. Do not expose the creature(s) to the air. They must remain fully submerge.

Use the tubing and establish a siphon drip line from the main tank into the bucket. Regulate the flow by tying loose knots in the tubing or using an airline control valve.

When the volume of the water in the bucket doubles, discard half the amount and begin the drip again. If your drip is running at the correct rate, this should take about one hour per fill.

When the water volume in the bucket doubles the second time, you are ready to transfer the life forms to the aquarium.

Again, do not expose invertebrates to the air. Scoop each creature out of the bucket gently with a specimen bag, then submerge the bag underwater in the tank.

Part II – Populating Your Saltwater Tank

Only when the bag is submerged can you gently remove the life form. Seal the bag underwater by twisting it closed. Remove it from the tank and discard both the bag and the water it contains.

If you are handling live coral, NEVER touch the "fleshy" part of the creature.

Dealing with Aggression

You may immediately be faced with a situation in which the new tank inhabitant is being chased and harassed by existing members of the population. An easy solution is to buy a plastic pasta strainer and give the bully a time out.

Simply float the bowl in the water, net the aggressive fish -- not the new arrival -- and put it in the bowl for four hours. The new arrival needs to get used to the tank and get over the stress of transport. The bully needs to learn how to mind his manners!

If the situation is proving more difficult to manage, you can use a divider temporarily that allow the two fish to see each other until the aggressive behavior subsides. These are typically issues of territoriality that sort themselves out.

Be prepared for the worst, however. Sometimes these squabbles do get messy. If, however, you've done your research in advance, you should be able to avoid these fatal confrontations.

Part II – Populating Your Saltwater Tank

Dividers are available in varying sizes in a price range of $10-$20 (£6.3-£13). If your tank is too large for this solution, you can also look at acrylic acclimatization boxes like the Reef Gently AccliMate Pro, retailing for $45 (£29). This unit is affixed to the side of the tank and allows for a more manageable separation.

Acclimatization Tips

Do not ignore the stipulation about turning off the tank lights and working in a dim room. Light stress can be very severe for marine animals.

Go through the entire process of acclimatization even if you think the creature you've purchased has died in transport. Many invertebrates and even some fish will revive during the transitional process.

Don't put an airstone in the bag. This does not help your new fish by providing more oxygen, but rather elevates the pH level of the water and can cause ammonia to spike to a lethal degree.

Especially when working with sponges, claims, scallops, and gorgonias, do not expose the creatures to the air.

Part III – Overview of Saltwater Tank Care

It cannot be stressed strongly enough that no two saltwater tanks are exactly alike. That is part of the fascination of this hobby for so many enthusiasts.

You are creating and administering a world whose parameters you will come to know and understand intimately.

You will develop set routines that fit your equipment, are suitable to your tank size and location, and that meet the needs of the population the aquarium houses. The following are intended as guidelines.

Part III – Overview of Saltwater Tank Care

If you are using a computerized tank management system, you'll have a great deal of help in monitoring conditions and knowing when certain tasks need to be performed.

If you are not, keep a written and dated record of everything you do to and for your fish and their world — their very existence depends on it!

Feeding Your Saltwater Fish

Depending on the composition of your tank's population, you will likely have a combination of carnivores, herbivores, and omnivores. Know your fish and pick your foods accordingly.

Carnivores

Your meat-eating fish need lots of protein in their diet, and they generally like to "hunt" for themselves. You can also use fresh, meaty seafood. For carnivores, you'll likely be using:

- brine shrimp
- table seafood (scallops, shrimp, mussels)
- glass shrimp
- copepods and amphipods
- feeder fish
- tubificid worms (black worms and red worms)

Part III – Overview of Saltwater Tank Care

Because prepared flake or pellet foods create less mess in the tank, these items are always staples in a saltwater aquarist's "kitchen." You can also use freeze dried and frozen foods, but be careful. The freezing and drying processes destroy much of the nutritional value.

Herbivores

Fish that eat vegetable matter will also eat meaty seafood in order to meet their protein needs. They tend to like small crustaceans, and may even accidentally consume these creatures while going after the plant matter that is their preferred diet. These items include:

- macroalgae growing in the tank
- macroalgae cultivated in a special grow box called a refugium
- prepared seaweed

There are also prepared flake, pellet, freeze-dried, and frozen foods for your herbivores, and many aquarists will use leafy greens like spinach and kale in their tank. (If you do this, be sure to clean up the leftovers after an hour or so to limit fouling of the water.)

Omnivores

Fortunately many saltwater fish are omnivores, and will happily feed on a combination of the items listed above. The important thing with any population of fish is to make

Part III – Overview of Saltwater Tank Care

certain they are getting adequate nutrition and a sufficiently varied diet.

Types of Fish Food

Prepared foods are far and away the preferred means of feeding saltwater fish. You will see a vast array of these products offered as:

- flakes
- pellets
- sheets
- freeze dried
- frozen

Of these, flakes are the most commonly used due to the ease with which they can be stored and fed.

Make sure you are buying saltwater flakes, however, as the use of freshwater food over an extended time will lead your marine population to become malnourished.

As an example of pricing, Ocean Nutrition Formula One Flake costs $3.49 (£2).

Some pellet foods are designed to sink, which are good for benthic or bottom dwellers, while the floating variety is attractive to those fish that like to feed on the surface.

Part III – Overview of Saltwater Tank Care

A typically priced sinking pellet like New Life Spectrum Marine Fish Formula is priced at $7.99 (£5) per 150 grams.

While you should not feed flakes or pellets exclusively, these foods should occupy a major place on the "menu" you offer to your fish. Look for foods that offer a combination of Spirulina, tubifex worms, fishmeal, and algae among other ingredients.

Sheet foods are often types of seaweed that can also be consumed by humans. A good example is nori kelp used to

Part III – Overview of Saltwater Tank Care

make many types of sushi. If there are no preservatives added, nori is also an excellent meal for your marine fish.

The most popular freeze-dried foods are krill, tubifex worms, and copepods. Frozen foods are often prepared with a specific species in mind and represent hard to find or highly specific dietary needs.

How and When to Feed

Overfeeding is a huge problem in all types of aquariums and is one of the biggest mistakes beginners make. All you're really doing is increasing the amount of work you'll have to put in to keep the tank clean and the water chemically stable. When in doubt, underfeed!

A good schedule to follow would be a small amount of a well-balanced flake food in the morning, with a mid-day "snack" of a sheet, freeze-dried, or frozen food at noon.

You can rotate the choice through an evening meal for the tank, and several times a week substitute live food as "supper."

Always know your population! Some species may need to be fed at specific times, or will require that the food be placed in close proximity. Coral and sessile invertebrates can't walk or swim over to get their "plate."

As you are initially stocking your tank, make notes about the dietary requirements of each species you introduce and

Part III – Overview of Saltwater Tank Care

then develop your feeding plan in terms of content, frequency, and amount.

Cleaning Chores and Maintenance

The necessary chores to keep a saltwater aquarium clean and operating efficiently depend on several factors, including, but not limited to:

- the size of the tank
- the type of filtration used

Part III – Overview of Saltwater Tank Care

- the tank inhabitants (type and number)
- frequency of feedings

In general terms, however, these are the routine tasks broken down my scheduling interval.

Throughout all these maintenance chores, remove any algae from the glass and decoration. If you have a good "cleaning crew" in place, you probably won't need to worry about this one.

Crabs, snails, starfish, and shrimp can greatly minimize on-going cleaning chores, but they must be carefully chosen to live peacefully with the other tank inhabitants. If you aren't careful, your fish will see your cleaning crew as their afternoon snack.

Daily Maintenance

Each day check all system components to make sure they are running properly. Get in the habit of listening to your tank. Often you will hear a problem before you will see it.

Check the salinity, water level, and temperature. Replace evaporated water with preconditioned water as needed. (If you have a top off system and a sump, make sure there's adequate conditioned water in the sump.)

Watch your fish and ascertain if any are behaving abnormally. Look for signs of disease. Early treatment and potential quarantine for sick fish can save your entire tank.

Part III – Overview of Saltwater Tank Care

Weekly / 10 Days

Plan on a 15-20% water change and a complete check of water parameters including pH, KH, nitrate, and nitrite levels. Rinse the filter with part of the old aquarium water to make sure you do nothing to harm the beneficial bacteria in the water.

Vacuum the sand or gravel at this time and remove any dead plants or other debris.

You should always read all materials provided with any filtration unit you are using and follow the manufacturer's suggested maintenance schedule.

Monthly

Conduct a more thorough inspection of all equipment elements and replace your filter media. At the time of installation, you should have familiarized yourself with the operator's manual for each element of your system.

Follow all recommended maintenance procedures and fit them into your upkeep schedule accordingly.

On a monthly basis you will also want to look at all items in your aquarium supplies that have expiration dates and replace anything that has passed the recommended usage limit.

Part III – Overview of Saltwater Tank Care

Dealing with Emergencies

In Part II, we discussed a backup generator as an optional item in your saltwater tank equipment list. Now that you understand more about what is required to design and stock a marine environment, you may see why "optional" is a relative term.

A power failure will deprive your tank of water movement, oxygenation, heating, and cooling and lead to the build-up of toxic chemicals in the water very quickly.

Without a back-up means of power, you could lose thousands of dollars in livestock and equipment if anything shorted out.

You cannot simply move a saltwater tank to a new location and plug everything back in. The bigger your tank, the more backup power becomes an absolute necessity.

By the same token, you need to consider the potential damage to your home if a tank shatters, is tipped over, or begins to leak. Depending on the location of the aquarium, the water damage could be catastrophic.

Not all homeowners policies will cover such events, and you may have to purchase a special rider or ancillary coverage to include incidents relative to your tank.

Part III – Overview of Saltwater Tank Care

You will likely not be able to protect the value of the livestock the aquarium contains, but you can at least protect the premises and potentially recoup any equipment losses.

Part III – Overview of Saltwater Tank Care

Part IV – Saltwater Fish Health

Aquarists are, for the most part, the only "doctors" their fish will ever see. Maintaining the long-term health of your population is very much a matter of superior husbandry, with a particular eye toward good acclimation and introduction protocols, and the creation of outstanding water conditions.

This does not, however, prevent disease or parasites from affecting your tank. Below is a broad overview of the most common health and treatment options with which saltwater aquarists deal. Use this material to build a solid foundation to safeguard the well being of your tank inhabitants.

Signs of Disease

Instinctively, fish try to behave in a normal fashion for as long as possible in the presence of disease rather than appear to be easy prey. There are clear signs of illness with which you should familiarize yourself, but you will have to be vigilant about watching your tank's population. Often even the most observant aquarist doesn't realize something is wrong until it's too late to help.

- loss of appetite

If a fish has just been introduced to a tank, it may not eat due to stress, but should adapt fairly quickly. If an established fish refuses to eat, however, that is not a good sign and is reason for close observation.

Part IV – Saltwater Fish Health

- discoloration

Some fish do enter a catatonic state if it's dark or if they are frightened, which should not be confused with actual, sustained color loss. When pigments fade and do not return within a few hours, be concerned.

- rubbing

If a fish begins to rub obsessively against any object in the tank, it could be trying to soothe a skin irritation or rid itself of a parasite.

- rapid breathing

When fish breath rapidly, their gills may be infested, irritated, or infected. Any of these issues can affect the rate of oxygen exchange. Water quality might be at the heart of the matter, so immediately check that aeration equipment is functioning and that ammonia levels have not spiked.

- minimal movement

Not all fish are active swimmers. You should know the activity profile for each species in your tank. If any fish remains in one spot for a prolonged period, or stays near the surface or the bottom, a problem may be present.

- clamping of the fins

Part IV – Saltwater Fish Health

Clamping means that the fins are held tightly against the body or in a flat position.

- a discharge of mucous

In addition to discharge from the eyes, mouth, gills, or anus, be aware of any specks, spots, or growths on the fins or skin.

- unusual droppings

While this is a more difficult sign to link to a specific individual, any evidence of undigested food passed in droppings or the presence of blood is a definite indicator of illness.

Your Tank's "First Aid" Kit

It is always better to be prepared for potential illnesses than to wait for something to happen. This should include, if possible, a stand-by quarantine tank with an established nitrogen cycle.

Removing diseased fish is one of the best ways to protect the overall health of the tank's population, but unless the secondary tank's water is pre-conditioned, the stress of the transfer can be lethal.

Make sure you have plenty of water testing kits, including an ability to test for copper, which can be the cause of

Part IV – Saltwater Fish Health

adverse reactions in many species. Maintain an assortment of medications that are within their expiration range.

(Check the dates and replace this items from time to time. Periodic replacement of medications is always less expensive than replacing a fish.)

Standard medications should include:

- Formalin 3, an all-purpose treatment for problems caused by bacteria, fungi, and parasites,

Aquarium Solutions Ich-X SW - 16 oz. / .5 liter, $12 / £7

- Cupramine, a copper-based treatment for marine itch and marine velvet. (Check for tolerances by species.)

Seachem Cupramine - 100 ml, $7 / £5

- Maracyn 2 (24 count powder packets $14 / £9) and Neomycin (NeoPlex, 10 grams, $6 /£4), which are antibacterial agents and Malachite Green (4 oz. / 113 grams, $3 / £2), which is an anti-fungal.

- Methylene Blue, used for freshwater dips. - 4 oz. / 113 grams, $3 / £2

- Praziquantel (US) and Piperazine or Fenbendazole (UK) dewormers (Products sell in a range from $5-$10 / £3-£6.)

Part IV – Saltwater Fish Health

(Note that having these items on hand does not mean you may not have to purchase other medications as indicated for specific diseases or conditions.)

Common Disease and Conditions

Most diseases and conditions in aquariums can be grouped by causal agents: parasites, bacterial and fungal, viral, and worm related.

Parasites

The following are some of the most commonly seen parasites in marine tanks. (Please note that this is not intended to serve as a comprehensive list.)

- Cryptocaryon irritans (Marine Itch)

The saltwater equivalent of white spot, Cryptocaryon irritans, causes minor respiratory distress, a loss of appetite, and some irritation of the skin due to the presence of white to gray nodules about the size of a pinhead.

The infection is highly contagious, and fatal within 3-5 days. Its life cycle is complicated and the organism will continue to spread until all the fish have died or the survivors have build-up immunity.

Treatment options include copper-based medications, hyposalinity, freshwater dips, and nitroimidazoles. If

Part IV – Saltwater Fish Health

possible, consult a marine veterinarian or a more season aquarist for advice.

(Hyposalinity is a process of reducing the specific gravity of the tank to the range of 1.009-1.010 for a period of four to six weeks. The initial process can be done without acclimation, but when returning the salinity to normal, increase by no more than 0.002 points per day.)

- Amyloodinium (Velvet)

This parasite begins at the gills with evident respiratory distress, and then progresses rapidly across the skin. The fish will rub against objects and swim in erratic patterns. If not treated with hyposalinity, death will occur in two days.

- Turbellarian (Black Itch)

Caused by one or more types of flatworm, Turbellarian is also known as "black itch." Dark spots appear on the skin, and the parasite can spread to invertebrates.

The best treatment option is a 30-60 minute formalin bath repeated every three days until all signs of infestation are gone.

Take water from the tank and mix it with formalin in a bucket to administer the treatment. Use an airstone in the bucket for good aeration.

Part IV – Saltwater Fish Health

Place the fish in the bath for the required period, then transfer it to a second bucket of tank water. Dilute and discard the formalin solution. The second bucket essentially "rinses" the fish to prevent formalin for entering the main tank.

Dose at 0.6 ML of formalin per gallon of water. Use formalin 37.5%. Always use gloves and eye protection when applying formalin, and discard the gloves when you are done. Take care not to splash formalin on your skin.

- Brooklynella

Brooklynella is caused by protozoa, with confection confined initially to the gills before spreading across the skin causing sloughing of cells and ulcers.

The fish will be lethargic, with obvious mucus secretions. Death can occur within 12 hours. Other signs include heavy breathing and cloudy eyes.

Formalin 3 is the only known treatment. (See dip instructions above under Turbellarian. Repeat once a day for five days to treat Brooklynella.)

Bacterial and Fungal Disease

Some of the more common bacterial and fungal diseases seen in saltwater fish include, but are not limited to:

- Internal Bacterial Infections

Part IV – Saltwater Fish Health

Fish with internal bacterial infections will exhibit visible bloody streaks or patches. They should be removed from the main tank and quarantined.

Feed the affected fish a medicated antibacterial food with tetracycline. Then use a medication like Maracyn 2 that targets gram-negative bacteria as these are the most common. If this proves ineffective, switch to Erythromycin. Use all medications in the manner and for the duration described on the packaging. Do not mix medications.

When changing to a different medication, do a partial water change. Do not discontinue treatment even if the fish looks better until the full course of recommended treatment has been fulfilled.

- Fin Rot

In almost all cases fins begin to look ragged and deteriorate as a result of physical abuse and/or poor quality water. Gram negative bacteria then exacerbates the damage.

The best option is to quarantine the fish and to treat it with an anti-bacterial medication.

- Pop Eye / Cloudy Eye

When the eye swells and / or becomes cloudy in appearance, the fish has either suffered physical damage or

Part IV – Saltwater Fish Health

is feeling the effects of poor water quality and a secondary bacterial infection (usually gram negative bacteria.)

Quarantine the affected fish in a separate tank and use an anti-bacterial medication. In good quality water, however, this condition usually resolves on its own.

If necessary, daily baths in 4 liters of water containing 1 ml of 10% Baytril solution can be used for five days. This medication will have to be obtained from a veterinarian with a prescription

- Fish Tuberculosis

Tuberculosis is a common condition in marine fish with lesions appearing on any organ. Symptoms include visible ulcerations, emaciation, anorexia, color loss, respiratory distress, or protruding eyes.

Since fish tuberculosis does present a potential danger to humans, a laboratory diagnosis is essential. Although treatment is possible, it is extremely difficult. In most cases, euthanizing the fish is kinder.

- External Bubble Disease

There can be multiple causes for this condition. If the bubbles appear to be filled with liquid, remove the fish to a quarantine tank and treat with antibiotics.

Part IV – Saltwater Fish Health

There is likely harmful bacterial growing in the main tank. Change out the substrate and thoroughly clean and service the filtration components.

If the bubbles are shiny, the water contains too many total dissolved gases, which can mean the water is too heavily aerated and overly warm. Slow down the rate of filtration and carefully regulate the temperature in the tank.

Viral Diseases

Although viruses are common in fish, not all are associated with actual outbreaks of disease. Unfortunately, when disease does occur, treatment with this class of illnesses is almost never practical.

You can make sure that the fish has the best conditions possible to allow its own immune system to work, and quarantine is always an option. Beyond that, in instances of viral infections, the aquarist has few courses of action.

- Lymphocyctis virus

When the Lymphocyctis virus is present, gray to white masses of cells will appear on the gills and fins, and may also be present in the body cavity and muscles.

The condition is easily confused with parasitic cysts and sarcomas, but the infection is typically self-limiting and will generally clear of its own accord in otherwise healthy specimens.

Part IV – Saltwater Fish Health

- Tang Fingerprint Disease

This disease will appear in both Tangs and Surgeon fish and is characterized by areas of discoloration on the sides that look like fingerprints. Under ideal conditions, the disease will resolve on its own, but death is not uncommon.

- Infectious Pancreatic Necrosis Virus

Fish with the Infectious Pancreatic Necrosis Virus become lethargic, stop eating, and show obvious disorientation. Some will bloat or show fluid accumulation and hemorrhages at the base of the fins.

- Angelfish Encephalitis

This condition is most common in French and Gray angelfish. Lethargy presents with loss of appetite and the presence of mucus. Eventually affected fish lose their balance completely and invariably die. There are no control measures or treatments.

- Head Lateral Line Erosion (HLLE)

Head Lateral Line Erosion begins with pitting or holes that develop around the eyes and down the lateral line. This is always a consequence of poor diet and poor water. Improving both will, in most cases, lead to a complete recovery.

Part IV – Saltwater Fish Health

Worm Infestations

The following are common worms in marine tanks, but please note that this is not an all-inclusive list.

- Turbellarian flatworms

These flatworms most frequently affect yellow tangs, surgeons, butterfly fish, parrot fish, and wrasse. Their presence indicates a poor level of maintenance and too much organic matter in the tank.

A thorough cleaning and water change are indicated, while fish should be treated with an anti-worming agent.

- Monogenean parasites

Commonly referred to as flukes and flatworms, Monogenean parasites typically infest the gills. They are passed fish to fish. Formalin baths will be required to kill adult parasites, but eggs can survive a single treatment.

The parasites cause skin ulcerations and, over time, can inflict painful and heavy damage, opening an opportunistic pathway for other pathogens and secondary infections. Use of a deworming agent and antibacterial medications is indicated.

Part IV – Saltwater Fish Health

- Monogenetic Trematodes

These parasites are most commonly seen near the eyes or gills and cause the fish to rub or scratch against objects in the tank and to exhibit heavy respiration. Fin clamping and hovering are also possible, as is eventual corneal ulceration and functional loss of vision.

Thankfully monogenetic trematodes are rare in marine tanks because their life cycle demands an intermediate host.

Medications and Treatments

In the discussion of conditions above, it becomes clear that there are only two approaches to treating fish disease:

- chemical based
- environmental

It is essential that treatments do not take place in the main tank. Although many beginning aquarists balk at having a quarantine tank after spending all the money for their initial set up, this secondary aquarium becomes essential over time for many reasons.

In truth, all new acquisitions should be placed in a quarantine tank first to protect your main population.

As a preventive for any disease or parasite, keep your water in absolutely prime condition and regulate temperatures into the lower 70 F (21 C) range to inhibit pathogen growth.

Part IV – Saltwater Fish Health

Also, PLEASE NOTE, if you are keeping scaleless fish, any medication for parasites (including cooper and formalin) must be used at half strength.

There are actually few of these that will be normally kept in a marine tank, but this can be an issue with eels and other elongated species.

A Word About Veterinarians

There are few veterinarians trained in the field of aquarium fish medicine. Some exotic vets have taken on a course of self-education on behalf of their clients, but in general, it is rare for a saltwater aquarist to have the advice of a veterinarian.

Most fish keepers learn to be their own vets. The Internet is an invaluable resource in this regard, connecting communities of saltwater aquarists all over the world. Information, photographs, and suggested treatment protocols are routinely traded in discussion forums.

In addition, there are many fine reference books specifically covering health issues specific to marine tanks. An example is, "The Marine Fish Health and Feeding Handbook: The Essential Guide to Keeping Saltwater Species Alive and Thriving" by Bob Goemans.

The longer you keep a saltwater aquarium, the more you will recognize the value of amassing a reference library and of keeping records on your fish. .

Part IV – Saltwater Fish Health

Treating your fish on your own may seem daunting at first, but as opposed to simply standing by and watching as they suffer, learning is a small matter.

Caring for your fish under all circumstances is simply part of the business of being an aquarist, and one that does become easier over time.

Part IV – Saltwater Fish Health

Afterword

You should now understand that keeping a saltwater aquarium represents high levels of commitment, both in terms of time and money. Marine aquarists are part chemist and part engineer.

They design intricate systems to maintain water quality while playing the role of aquatic diplomats, striving to create peaceful communities of creatures that are not only beautiful, but that can thrive in the closed tank environment.

Saltwater tanks are big, and they are not inexpensive. This has both advantages and disadvantages. You need a solid budget, adequate room with sound structural integrity, and a lot of time to set everything up and maintain it properly. Your investment in livestock, with some fish selling for hundreds of dollars, demands nothing less.

Only you can decide if you have all the resources necessary to keep a saltwater tank. It is not a decision to be made on the spur of the moment, or without adequate research and preparation.

If you visit saltwater discussion forums online, you will quickly see the seasoned veterans mentoring new members and answering their seemingly endless array of questions.

This is not, by any means, an impossible or inaccessible hobby, but it is a demanding one, and not for everyone.

Afterword

This text was designed to give you a solid foundation, one on which you will hopefully continue to build for many years to come. Your reward will be a living piece of art in your home or office that is an expression of your skill and expertise.

Why do people keep any kind of aquarium? Because the underwater world of our planet's oceans fascinates us. We can visit those depths, but we cannot live there.

We can, however, with care, bring the smallest part of that vast world into our lives in the beautifully cultivated microcosm of a saltwater aquarium.

Relevant Websites

Pet Fish Talk
"How to Start Your First Saltwater Aquarium: An Interview with Even from Colorado."
www.petfishtalk.com/interviews/saltwater/saltwater.htm

The Aquarium 101 - Your Aquarium Info Center
www.theaquarium101.com/tips-keeping-saltwater-fish/

Successfully Set Up a Saltwater Aquarium - Melev's Reef
www.melevsreef.com/overview.htm

Reef Aquarium Forum
www.reefland.com

Fish Channel - All Saltwater Species
www.fishchannel.com/fish-species/saltwater_all_landing.aspx

Fishlore - Aquarium Fish Information
"Saltwater Aquarium Fish Guide for Saltwater Fish"
www.fishlore.com/SaltwaterBeginners.htm

Saltwater Aquarium Online Guide
www.saltwater-aquarium-online-guide.com

Beginner Saltwater Invertebrates
www.saltwateraquariumsupplies.org/beginner-saltwater-invertebrates

Relevant Websites

A Beginner's Guide to Setting Up a Large Marine Tank
www.fishkeeping.co.uk/articles_29/large-marine-tank-setup.htm

Corals for Your Saltwater Aquarium: A Photo Guide
idiotsguides.com/static/quickguides/pets/corals-for-your-saltwater-aquarium-a-photo-guide.html

Reef Cleaners - Beginner's Guide
www.reefcleaners.org/index.php?option=com_content&view=article&id=46&Itemid=59

Frequently Asked Questions

Frequently Asked Questions

To truly appreciate all that is involved in keeping a saltwater or marine aquarium, you are encouraged to read the entirety of this text. The following are, however, some questions most frequently asked by individuals considering taking up the hobby.

Do saltwater aquariums take a lot of work?

The short answer is, yes. Any aquarium, if kept properly, is labour intensive. At the same time, however, if you love maintaining the integrity of a closed environment and supporting the life forms it houses, aquaculture is also an absorbing and fascinating pastime.

Many people choose saltwater tanks for that very reason, as they find maintaining water chemistry and successfully intermingling fish species to be intriguing challenges. There are more homes in the United States with aquariums than with dogs and cats.

Before undertaking the creation of a saltwater tank, it's imperative to become thoroughly educated and preferably to make the acquaintance off more experienced aquarists — either in person or online. Having mentors to whom you can turn is an invaluable resource.

When you do achieve a well-designed and beautiful tank, you have a living piece of art, and one whose inhabitants

Frequently Asked Questions

you will come to care about far more than you may realize in the beginning.

Am I going to create a lot of humidity in my house? Will a big tank leak or spill alot?

Evaporation will be present in any tank, which is why one of the recommended pieces of equipment is an auto top off system. The amount of evaporation is not, however, sufficient to elevate the humidity in the surrounding room, much less the whole house.

It is a good idea with large aquariums to have an overflow box in the event of a leak or other catastrophe that could inject large amount of water into the room.

You might also consider talking to your insurance agent about adding a rider to your homeowners policy to cover such damage. These events are rare, but taking extra precautions will give you more peace of mind.

Why is tank size such a big deal? Don't fish just grow to whatever size is right for the tank and stop?

The idea that fish grow according to available space is not only a huge myth, but it's also rather ridiculous. All fish have a maximum physical length and a recommended minimum tank volume for both their eventual size and activity profile. You should pay serious attention to both, and stock your aquarium accordingly.

Frequently Asked Questions

As a beginner, shouldn't I start out small?

Small isn't actually such a great idea when you're taking saltwater tanks. This recommended size this text suggests is 180 gallons (681.37 liters).

With a tank of this size, you'll have greater freedom to stock the aquarium with interesting fish, and a much easier time of maintaining good water chemistry, a crucial element in fish husbandry.

Is there really that much differences in saltwater and freshwater tanks?

The major difference is in the origin of the fish themselves. Freshwater fish tend to be tank or pond raised and thus more tolerant of fluctuating water chemistry. Many saltwater fish are captured in the wild and are extremely sensitive.

For this reason, saltwater tanks are more challenging for beginners, but they are certainly not impossible, especially if you are someone who enjoys detailed hobbies.

Just how hard are saltwater tanks?

The hardest part in any tank is water chemistry, followed by building a workable community of tank mates. Population management with marine species must be carefully planned to avoid predation and stress.

Frequently Asked Questions

Your issues as a "landlord" will extend to matters of size, temperament, personality, and diet among other factors. Assessing compatibility and working with size estimates to stay within recommended norms is crucial.

What do I have to consider in terms of tank location? Can I put my saltwater aquarium in front of a window?

In terms of tank placement, think about the weight of the tank first. Do your math. A gallon of water weighs 8 lbs. (3.628 kg), so a 180 gallon (681.37 liter) tank will weigh 1,440 lbs. or 653.17 kg.

Placing any tank in front of a window is not a good idea because the water will not only become too warm, but you'll get uncontrolled algae growth.

Can you give me any idea of where it's safe to put a tank of that size in my house without the floor caving in?

A 100 gallon (378.54 liter) tank can be placed just about anywhere, but from 100 to 220 gallons (378.54 to 832.79 liters), the tank should sit along a load-bearing wall perpendicular to the floor joists.

Should you go larger, into the 220 to 400 gallon (832.79 to 1514.16 liter) range, it will be necessary to place the aquarium on a reinforced floor. Above 400 gallons (1514.16 liters)? The tank will have to be placed directly on a concrete slab.

Frequently Asked Questions

What is the difference in a "fish" tank and a "reef" tank?

A "fish" tank is easy. It just contains fish. There is actually an intermediate arrangement called a FOWLR aquarium — "Fish Only With Live Rock." That means there's living coral in the tank as well.

A reef aquarium, on the other hand, contains a carefully planned population of peaceful fish co-existing with creatures like shrimp, anemones, crabs, sponges, snails, urchins, shrimp, starfish, crabs, and duster worms.

How much electricity does a big tank use?

To get an accurate calculation, you will have to keep actual usage records that reflect your local cost of electricity and the efficiency of your equipment. Using LED lights will certainly cut down on costs. The lights will run 8-12 hours a day.

For a 90 gallon tank (340.687 liters) that will require about 400-600 watts a day for the essential equipment, with the lighting adding another 200-700 watts. (These calculations can, however, vary widely.)

Can a saltwater tank be converted to freshwater?

A conversion from freshwater to saltwater is possible, but practically, it's more cost effective to start a new tank. By the time you've bought new equipment and cycled the

Frequently Asked Questions

saltwater, which can take up to two months, you won't have saved any money.

You also have to decide what to do with your freshwater fish. Many aquarists run side-by-side fresh and saltwater tanks and thoroughly enjoy the added variety.

Should I buy a glass tank or one made of acrylic?

As a rule of thumb, aquariums 300 gallons (1,135 liters) and under are built of glass. The material is cheaper, and these tanks tend to come in standard "off the shelf" sizes and configurations.

From 300 gallons and up, tanks are typically custom designed and made of acrylic. The material is lighter and clearer, but it is expensive, and does scratch more easily. Acrylic is, however, more flexible in terms of fabrication options.

Glossary

A

acidity - The pH level of the water is one of the most common quality measurements taken. It is not as crucial as the amount of toxic ammonia present in a tank, but is a variable that should be monitored and kept within the recommended range.

actinic lights - These blue spectrum lights use fluorescent bulbs to recreate the quality of ocean light at a depth of approximately 30 feet. Although there are other kinds of lights now commonly used in saltwater tanks, actinics are still typically used in reef tanks.

activated carbon - This is an absorbent carbon-based material used in filtration systems. Activated carbon will not remove either ammonia or nitrite, nor does it work to soften the water. It is useful, however, in the control of organic matter in the water.

air pump - The generic term for the devices used in any type of aquarium that serve to aerate or oxygenate the water.

algae scraper - As the name implies, this is a tool that facilitates the mass removal of algae growth from the glass or acrylic sides of an aquarium.

Glossary

algae - The catch-all term "algae" covers an extensive collection of aquatic plants that proliferate as nuisance growth in aquariums.

alkalinity - This somewhat confusing measurement refers to the capacity of water to act as a buffer. The measurement addresses the ability of the water to neutralize acid without creating a dip in pH levels.

ammonia - This is the major and most deadly toxin that accumulates in aquarium water as a consequence of fish excrement. Ammonia must be neutralized by the establishment of the nitrogen cycle in the tank, a life cycle of beneficial bacteria working in concert to create water capable of sustaining marine life.

anoxia - A state in which no oxygen is present.

aquaculture - The practice of cultivating aquatic lifeforms as a source of food or for pleasure.

aquascaping - The aesthetic arrangement of elements in an aquarium including the selection of inhabitants, with a goal of creating an authentic underwater environment.

aquarist - The keeper of an aquarium.

aquatic plant - Any plant that will grow fully or partially submerged in water.

Glossary

B

beneficial bacteria - Bacteria introduced into an aquarium through the establishment of the nitrogen cycle that work to convert toxic ammonia into relatively harmless nitrate.

benthic - Living in or occurring in the bottom level of a body of water or in an aquarium.

C

carbonate hardness - The measurement of water's ability to absorb and neutralize acid. One of the important factors of water quality in an aquarium.

carbon dioxide (CO_2) - The respiration of animals and plants (during photosynthesis) creates this odorless, colorless gas.

chiller - A device in an aquarium's life support system that function to lower water temperature.

chlorination - To make water safer for human consumption, municipal water systems add the purification agent chlorine. Only de-chlorinated water should be used in aquariums.

cycling - In cycling a tank, beneficial bacteria are established to work in the nitrogen cycle for the purpose of converting toxic ammonia to nitrates, thus rendering the water capable of supporting marine life.

Glossary

D

deionization (DI) - During this process, water is purified by the use of ion exchange resins working with activated carbon and a bacterial filter. The system removes 100% of inorganic chemicals.

detritus - Any dead material of a bacterial, plant, or animal nature, which, through bacterial processes, can be degraded.

E

ecosystem - A community of organisms interacting with the physical environment which they inhabit.

F

fluorescent light - Light fixtures used in aquariums to supply low cost, broad spectrum illumination.

G

glass aquarium - Standard sized aquariums routinely sold in pet stores are typically made of glass, while high-volume customized tanks are generally constructed from acrylic.

H

hang on the back filter - As the name implies, a filter hanging off the back of the aquarium outfitted with a draw

Glossary

tube to carry water through the mechanism to be filtered and returned to the tank.

heater - A device for the control of water temperature, typically a glass tube, used in an aquarium. Generally accurate to within 2 degrees of the target level.

herbivore - Animals that eat plants as their staple food source.

hydrometer - A device that is used to determine a fluid's specific gravity or salinity.

I

invertebrate - Aquarium animals lacking spines. Examples might be starfish, clams, worms, and crabs.

L

lateral line - Perforated scales running in a line along a fish's flank that are sensitive to vibrations in the water.

live rock - Rock or coral seeded with marine organisms and used in aquariums as both decorative material and biological filtration. They serve as the focal point of reef tanks.

Glossary

N

nitrification - A bacteriological process that serves to convert ammonia to nitrate and then in turn changes the nitrite to nitrate.

O

omnivore - Animals that consume both plants and other animals for food.

P

predator - Animals that prey on other animal for food.

R

reverse osmosis (RO) - A process of water purification utilizing high pressure and selective membranes. RO will take out 100% of bacteria and 85% to 95% of inorganic chemicals present.

S

salinity - The level of dissolved salts present in water.

specific gravity - The measurement of the degree of salt present in aquarium water at any give time.

substrate - The material lining the bottom of an aquarium. In saltwater tanks, sand is most often used.

Glossary

sump - A container or box, usually with a water reservoir attached, that serves as an equipment storage area.

T

territorial - An expression of actual or perceptual ownership of a chosen area in the surrounding environment. A behavior exhibited by many marine species.

W

water quality - The chemical composition and stability of aquarium water, and a crucial element of tank husbandry.

Glossary

Index

Index
50/50 bulbs, 22
acrylic, 18, 80
actinic element, 22
aggression, 39
airstone, 80, 99
algae, 20
alkalinity, 31
ammonia, 25, 31, 32, 34, 35, 80
Amyloodinium, 99
Angelfish Encephalitis, 104
aquarist, 12, 84
aquarium, 1, 12, 14, 17, 19, 21, 22, 25, 27, 29, 30, 34, 35, 39, 42, 46, 47, 76, 78, 82, 88, 90, 91, 92
auto top off system, 30
backup generator, 28, 91
bacteria, 16, 34, 35, 90
Banded-Tail Coral-Cod, 50
Banggai Cardinal Fish, 46
barbels, 48
beginners, 40, 76, 87
beneficial bacteria, 34
Bigeye Soldierfish, 50
Black Itch, 99
Blackbar Soldierfish, 51
Blue Green Chromis, 45
Blue Spot Rock Cod, 49
body, 43, 46, 48, 50, 53, 54
brine shrimp, 83
Brooklynella, 100
bull-bottom support, 18
calcium, 33
carbon blocks, 21
carbonate hardness, 31
carnivores, 44, 46, 48, 49, 83
Chainlink Moray Eel, 48
chemical testing kits, 25
chiller, 24, 30
chlorine, 20, 21
clamping of the fins, 95
climate control, 25
Cloudy Eye, 101
Clownfish, 13, 45
computer-based sensors, 25
contaminants, 21
coral, 15, 21, 23, 24, 42, 48, 75, 77, 79
Coral Hind, 49
crustaceans, 84
Cryptocaryon irritans, 98
Damselfish, 34, 44
Darkfinned Hind, 50
dead base rock, 23
de-chlorination, 20

Index

DI cartridge, 21
dietary needs, 44, 87
discharge of mucous, 96
discoloration, 95, 104
dorsal fin, 51
Dwarf / Zebra Lionfish, 53
eels, 47, 48, 49
eggs, 105
electricity, 24
energy efficient, 22, 24
External Bubble Disease, 102
eyes, 43, 52
feeder fish, 46, 83
fertilizers, 20
Fin Rot, 101
fins, 43, 46, 50, 51, 53
Firefish, 45, 46, 54
Fish only aquariums, 15
fish only tank, 15
Fish Tuberculosis, 102
flow rate, 19
freeze-dried, 84, 87
frozen food, 87
fungus, 43
gallons per hour (GPH), 19
Ghost eel, 47
groupers, 49
growths, 43

Head Lateral Line Erosion (HLLE), 104
heater, 24, 30
humidity, 114
hyposalinity, 98, 99
Infectious Pancreatic Necrosis Virus, 104
inshore rock, 23
Internal Bacterial Infections, 100
invertebrates, 16, 17, 21, 42, 50, 75, 78, 80, 87
iodine, 33
Kaudern's Cardinals, 46
kelp, 86
Large Tail or Military Turkey Fish, 54
LED lights, 22
lighting, 16, 17, 22
Lionfish, 53, 54
liters per hour (LPH), 19
live rock, 15, 16, 22, 24
Long-Finned Cardinal Fish, 46
loss of appetite, 94, 98, 104
Lymphocystis virus, 103
macroscopic organisms, 22
magnesium, 33
Marine Itch, 98
Miniatus Grouper, 49, 50

Index

minimal movement, 95
Monogenean parasites, 105
Monogenetic Trematodes, 106
nitrate, 32, 34, 90
nitrates, 20, 25, 35
nitrogen cycle, 33
nitroimidazoles, 98
nori, 86
omnivores, 44, 45, 83, 84
overflow box, 29
pesticides, 20
pH, 19, 27, 31, 32, 76, 80, 90
pharmaceuticals, 20
phosphate, 32
phosphates, 20, 25
photosynthetic, 17
Plain Tail Firefish, 54
Pop Eye, 101
Popeye Cataluta Soldierfish, 50
Porcupine Puffer, 53
power failure, 29, 91
power of hydrogen, 31
powerheads, 19, 30
protein skimmers, 19
Protein skimmers, 18
Puffers, 52
rapid breathing, 95

Red Flag Grouper, 49, 50
Red Volitans, 53
reef tank, 15, 17, 22
reef tanks, 16
refractometer, 25, 31
refugium, 84
Reverse Osmosis De-Ionization (RODI), 20
RO membrane, 21
rubbing, 95
Russell's Lionfish, 53
salinity, 2, 25, 27, 31, 32, 76, 89
salt, 20, 43
sand, 24, 90
scaleless fish, 107
seaweed, 23, 56, 84, 86
secondary filtration, 16
sediment filter, 21
Snowflake eel, 47, 48
Soldier Lionfish, 53
Soldierfish, 50, 51
specific gravity, 31, 32, 76
sponges, 16, 23, 42, 80
Spotted Grouper, 49, 50
Stars and Stripes Puffer, 52
strontium, 33
substrate, 30
sump, 27, 30, 89
supplements, 16

Index

Tang Fingerprint Disease, 104
tank size, 12, 14, 18, 19, 82
tap water, 20
tubificid worms, 83
Turbellarian, 99, 100, 105
Turbellarian flatworms, 105
turnover rate, 19
unusual droppings, 96
Velvet, 99
veterinarians, 107
V-Tailed Grouper, 50
Waste materials, 18
water chemistry, 1, 15, 44, 75, 113, 115
water level, 27, 28, 89
water movement, 19, 91
weight, 12, 17
worms, 83, 86, 87, 105, 123

www.ingramcontent.com/pod-product-compliance
Lightning Source LLC
Chambersburg PA
CBHW060836050426
42453CB00008B/720